Houghton Mifflin Reading
A Legacy of Literacy

Kindergarten

Teacher's Edition

Senior Authors J. David Cooper, John J. Pikulski

Authors Patricia A. Ackerman, Kathryn H. Au, David J. Chard, Gilbert G. Garcia, Claude N. Goldenberg, Marjorie Y. Lipson, Susan E. Page, Shane Templeton, Sheila W. Valencia, MaryEllen Vogt

Consultants Linda H. Butler, Linnea C. Ehri, Carla B. Ford

HOUGHTON MIFFLIN

BOSTON • MORRIS PLAINS, NJ

California • Colorado • Georgia • Illinois • New Jersey • Texas

Literature Reviewers

Consultants: **Dr. Adela Artola Allen**, Associate Dean, Graduate College, Associate Vice President for Inter-American Relations, University of Arizona, Tucson, Arizona; **Dr. Manley Begay**, Co-director of the Harvard Project on American Indian Economic Development, Director of the National Executive Education Program for Native Americans, Harvard University, John F. Kennedy School of Government, Cambridge, Massachusetts; **Dr. Nicholas Kannellos**, Director, Arte Publico Press, Director, Recovering the U.S. Hispanic Literacy Heritage Project, University of Houston, Texas; **Mildred Lee**, author and former head of Library Services for Sonoma County, Santa Rosa, California; **Dr. Barbara Moy**, Director of the Office of Communication Arts, Detroit Public Schools, Michigan; **Norma Naranjo**, Clark County School District, Las Vegas, Nevada; **Dr. Arlette Ingram Willis**, Associate Professor, Department of Curriculum and Instruction, Division of Language and Literacy, University of Illinois at Urbana-Champaign, Illinois

Teachers: **Helen Brooks**, Vestavia Hills Elementary School, Birmingham, Alabama; **Patricia Buchanan**, Thurgood Marshall School, Newark, Delaware; **Gail Connor**, Language Arts Resource Teacher, Duval County, Jacksonville, Florida; **Vicki DeMott**, McClean Science/Technology School, Wichita, Kansas; **Marge Egenhoffer**, Dixon Elementary School, Brookline, Wisconsin; **Mary Jew Mori**, Griffin Avenue Elementary, Los Angeles, California

Program Reviewers

Supervisors: **Judy Artz**, Middletown Monroe City School District, Ohio; **James Bennett**, Elkhart Schools, Elkhart, Indiana; **Kay Buckner-Seal**, Wayne County, Michigan; **Charlotte Carr**, Seattle School District, Washington; **Sister Marion Christi**, St. Matthews School, Archdiocese of Philadelphia, Pennsylvania; **Alvina Crouse**, Garden Place Elementary, Denver Public Schools, Colorado; **Peggy DeLapp**, Minneapolis, Minnesota; **Carol Erlandson**, Wayne Township Schools, Marion County, Indianapolis; **Brenda Feeney**, North Kansas City School District, Missouri; **Winnie Huebsch**, Sheboygan Area Schools, Wisconsin; **Brenda Mickey**, Winston-Salem/Forsyth County Schools, North Carolina; **Audrey Miller**, Sharpe Elementary School, Camden, New Jersey; **JoAnne Piccolo**, Rocky Mountain Elementary, Adams 12 District, Colorado; **Sarah Rentz**, East Baton Rouge Parish School District, Louisiana; **Kathy Sullivan**, Omaha Public Schools, Nebraska; **Rosie Washington**, Kuny Elementary, Gary, Indiana; **Theresa Wishart**, Knox County Public Schools, Tennessee

Teachers: **Carol Brockhouse**, Madison Schools, Wayne Westland Schools, Michigan; **Eva Jean Conway**, R.C. Hill School, Valley View School District, Illinois; **Carol Daley**, Jane Addams School, Sioux Falls, South Dakota; **Karen Landers**, Watwood Elementary, Talladega County, Alabama; **Barb LeFerrier**, Mullenix Ridge Elementary, South Kitsap District, Port Orchard, Washington; **Loretta Piggee**, Nobel School, Gary, Indiana; **Cheryl Remash**, Webster Elementary School, Manchester, New Hampshire; **Marilynn Rose**, Michigan; **Kathy Scholtz**, Amesbury Elementary School, Amesbury, Massachusetts; **Dottie Thompson**, Erwin Elementary, Jefferson County, Alabama; **Dana Vassar**, Moore Elementary School, Winston-Salem, North Carolina; **Joy Walls**, Ibraham Elementary School, Winston-Salem, North Carolina; **Elaine Warwick**, Fairview Elementary, Williamson County, Tennessee

Credits

Cover and Theme Opener
Corbis Royalty-Free Images

Assignment Photography
Joel Benjamin
pp. xiv, T6, T13, T21, T23, T34, T45, T60, T69, T77, T79, T90, T101, T125, T133, T135, T151

Illustration
p. T67, copyright © 2001 by John Sandford; Sonja Lamut, p. T123

Acknowledgments

Grateful acknowledgment is made for permission to reprint copyrighted material as follows:

Theme 3
Tortillas and Lullabies/Tortillas y Cancionitas, by Lynn Whisnant Reiser. Illustrations by "Corazones Valientes." Text copyright © 1998 by Lynn Whisnant Reiser. Illustrations copyright © 1998 by "Corazones Valientes." Reprinted by arrangement with Greenwillow Books, a division of William Morrow & Company Inc.

Shoes from Grandpa, by Mem Fox, illustrated by Patricia Mullins. Text copyright © 1989 by Mem Fox. Illustrations copyright © 1989 by Patricia Mullins. All rights reserved. Reprinted by permission of Orchard Books, New York.

Our Family

Mom & Dad

Brother

We're a Family!

OBJECTIVES

Phonemic Awareness beginning sounds

Phonics sounds for letters *T, t; B, b; N, n*

High-Frequency Words recognize two new high-frequency words

Reading Strategies evaluate; predict/infer; summarize; phonics/decoding

Comprehension Skills story structure: characters and setting; inferences: drawing conclusions

Vocabulary movement words; family words; exact naming words; types of clothing; action words; order words

Writing recording observation; journal entry; grocery list; choosing a good title; order words

Listening/Speaking/Viewing activities to support vocabulary expansion and writing

Theme 3

We're a Family
Literature Resources

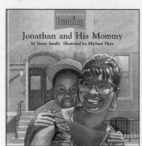

Big Books for Use All Year

From Apples to Zebras: A Book of ABC's

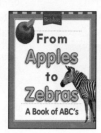

Higglety Pigglety: A Book of Rhymes

Leveled Books

See Cumulative Listing of Leveled Books.

Phonics Library

Decodable

- The Birthday Party
- Baby Bear's Family
- Cat's Surprise

Lessons, pages T37, T93, T143

On My Way Practice Reader

Easy / **On Level**

Nicky Takes a Bath
by Sam Fonte
page T157

Little Big Books

On Level / **Challenge**

Tortillas and Lullabies

Shoes from Grandpa

📼 Audiotape

We're a Family

Houghton Mifflin Classroom Bookshelf

Level K

Little Readers for Guided Reading

Collection K

Theme 3

Bibliography

Books for Browsing

 Lots of Dads
by Shelley Rotner
Dial 1997 (32p)
Photographs show all kinds of dads engaged in activities from work to play with their children.

 Bath Time
by Lucy Malka
Lee & Low 2000 (8p)
A Latino boy puts so many things into his tub at bathtime that the water overflows.

Mothers Are Like That
by Carol Carrick
Clarion 2000 (28p)
Simple text describes how animals and human mothers care for their young.

 Mothers & Babies
by the World Wildlife Fund
Cedco 1997 (28p)
Labeled photographs show animal mothers and their babies.

 Buzz
by Janet S. Wong
Harcourt 2000 (32p)
A busy morning for an Asian American boy and his parents begins with the alarm clock's buzz.

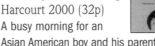

Mom and Me
by Miela Ford
Greenwillow 1998 (24p)
Photographs and brief text show a polar bear cub and its mother sleeping, playing, and eating at the zoo.

A High Low Near Far Loud Quiet Story
by Nina Crews
Greenwillow 1999 (24p)
Captioned photos show a sister and brother acting out a series of opposites during their day.

  Daddy Calls Me Man
by Angela Johnson
Orchard 1997 (32p)
A boy's artist parents inspire him to create four brief poems about his family.

 Bird Families
by Helen Frost
Pebble 1999 (24p)
Photographs and brief, repetitive text describe where and how cardinals, puffins, and other birds nest.

Books for Teacher Read Aloud

Big Book of Families
by Catherine and Laurence Anholt
Candlewick 1998 (32p)
Rhyming poems and pictures celebrate all kinds of families.

Katy No-Pocket *
by Emmy Payne
Houghton (32p) also paper
Pocketless Katy Kangaroo sets out to find something in which to carry her son, Freddy. **Available in Spanish as** *Katy no tiene bolsa.*

Rabbit Food
by Susanna Gretz
Candlewick 1999 (32p)
Uncle Bunny tries to get his nephew John to eat the carrots and celery that he himself dislikes.

 A Birthday Basket for Tía
by Pat Mora
Simon 1992 (32p) also paper
A girl gathers a basket full of special things for her great-aunt's birthday. **Available in Spanish as** *Una canasta de cumpleañños para Tía.*

When Will Sarah Come?
by Elizabeth Fitzgerald Howard
Greenwillow 1999 (32p)
Jonathan, an African American boy, waits impatiently for his sister Sarah to come home from school.

 On Mother's Lap *
by Ann Herbert Scott
Clarion 1992 (32p)
also paper
An Inuit boy discovers there's room for himself and his baby sister on their mother's lap.

Night Shift Daddy
by Eileen Spinelli
Hyperion 2000 (32p)
In rhyming text, a father shares dinner and bedtime rituals with his daughter before working the night shift.

Little Bear's Visit
by Else Holmelund Minarik
Harper 1961 (64p) also paper
Little Bear's favorite thing about visiting his grandparents is the stories they tell.

Come Along, Daisy!
by Jane Simmons
Little 1998 (32p)
Daisy the duckling forgets to follow her mama as she investigates the wildlife on her pond.

 Jamaica Tag-Along *
by Juanita Havill
Houghton 1989 (32p)
also paper
Jamaica's feelings are hurt when her brother won't let her tag along to his basketball game.

Under the Table
by Marisabina Russo
Greenwillow 1997 (32p)
A girl draws on the under side of a coffee table, and finds there are limits to what's allowed.

* = Included in Houghton Mifflin Classroom Bookshelf, Level K

Key

 Science

 Social Studies

 Multicultural

 Music

 Math

 Classic

 Art

Peter's Chair
by Ezra Jack Keats
Harper 1967 (32p) also paper
Peter learns to accept—and even to love—his new baby sister.
Available in Spanish as *La silla de Pedro.*

Books for Shared Reading

Off We Go!
by Jane Yolen
Little 2000 (32p)
In a rhythmic, rhyming story, Little Mouse, Little Frog, and other baby animals sing their way to grand-ma's house.

Big Brother, Little Brother
by Penny Dale
Candlewick 1997 (32p)
Two brothers know exactly how to help each other out when one of them is upset.

Does a Kangaroo Have a Mother, Too?
by Eric Carle
Harper 2000 (32p)
Through repetitive questions, read-ers learn that animals have moth-ers just like people do.

We're Making Breakfast for Mother
by Shirley Neitzel
Greenwillow 1997 (32p)
In a cumulative, rhyming rebus story, two children make break-fast—and a mess—for their mother.

Mama Cat Has Three Kittens
by Denise Fleming
Holt 1998 (32p)
While two kittens copy everything their mama does, their brother Boris naps.

 Hush, Little Baby
by Marla Frazee
Harper 1999 (32p)
In a lively interpretation of a tradi-tional Appalachian lullaby, a girl is sure she can calm a howling infant.

Books for Phonics Read Aloud

 New Moon
by Pegi Deitz Shea
Boyds Mills 1996 (32p)
A boy and his baby sister spend time watching the winter moon in the sky.

The Biggest Bed in the World
by Lindsay Camp
Harper 2000 (32p)
To get a good night's sleep, Ben's dad decides to build the biggest bed in the world.

No, No, Titus!
by Claire Masurel
North-South 1997 (32p) also paper
A farm family's dog has trouble fig-uring out exactly what his job is.

Bear's Busy Family
by Stella Blackstone
Barefoot 1999 (32p)
In simple rhyming text, a bear introduces and describes all of his relatives.

Technology

Computer Software Resources

- *Curious George® Learns Phonics*
- *Lexia Quick Reading Test*
- *Lexia Phonics Based Reading*
- *Published by Sunburst Technology**
   Tenth Planet™ Vowels: Short and Long
   Curious George® Pre-K ABCs
   First Phonics
- *Published by The Learning Company*
   Dr. Seuss's ABC™

*©Sunburst Technology Corporation, a Houghton Mifflin Comapny. All Rights Reserved.

Video Cassettes

- *A Birthday Basket for Tía by Pat Mora. Spoken Arts*
- *Owen by Kevin Henkes. Spoken Arts*
- *Hi Daddy. Blackboard Entertainment*
- *Blueberries for Sal by Robert McCloskey. Weston Woods*
- *Noisy Nora by Rosemary Wells. Weston Woods*

Audio Cassettes

- *Pig Pig Grows Up by David McPhail. Live Oak*
- *Rachel Fister's Blister by Amy McDonald. Houghton*
- *Where Are You Going, Little Mouse? by Robert Kraus. Listening Library*
- *Little Bear's Visit by Else Holmelund Minarik. Weston Woods*
- *The Mother's Day Mice by Eve Bunting. Houghton*
- *Katy No-Pocket by Emmy Payne. Houghton*
- *On Mother's Lap by Ann Herbert Scott. Houghton*
- *Audio Tapes for We're a Family. Houghton Mifflin Company.*

A-V addresses available on pages 00-00

Education Place
www.eduplace.com *log on to Education Place for more activities relating to We're a Family.*

Book Adventure
www.bookadventure.com *This Internet read-ing incentive program provides thousands of titles for students to read.*

* = Included in Houghton Mifflin Classroom Bookshelf, Level K

Theme 3

Theme at a Glance

Theme Concept: *Families work, play, and celebrate together.*

✓ **Indicates Tested Skills**

Learning to Read

	Phonemic Awareness and Phonics	High-Frequency Words	Comprehension Skills and Strategies
WEEK 1 **Read Aloud** **Jonathan and His Mommy** **Big Book** **Tortillas and Lullabies** **Social Studies Link** **Families** **Phonics Library** *"The Birthday Party"* 	✓ Phonemic Awareness: Beginning Sounds, *T9, T17, T27, T41, T49* ✓ Initial Consonant *t, T12–T13, T20–T21* ✓ Review Initial Consonant *t, T36, T44–T45* Phonics Review: Familiar Consonants; *m, s, t, T13, T20, T38, T46, T52, T54*	✓ High-Frequency Words, *T22–T23, T37, T53* **Word Wall**, *T8, T16, T26, T40, T48*	✓ Comprehension: Story Structure: Characters/Setting, *T10, T18, T29, T31, T50* **Strategies: Evaluate,** *T10, T18, T29, T32, T42* **Phonics/Decoding,** *T37*
WEEK 2 **Read Aloud** **Goldilocks and the Three Bears** **Big Book** **Shoes From Grandpa** **Social Studies Link** **Which Would You Choose?** **Phonics Library** *"Baby Bear's Family"* 	✓ Phonemic Awareness: Beginning Sounds, *T63, T73, T83, T97, T105* ✓ Initial Consonant *b, T68–T69, T76–T77* ✓ Review Initial Consonant *b, T92, T100–T101* Phonics Review: Familiar Consonants; *b, m, r, t, T69, T76, T94, T102, T108, T110*	✓ High-Frequency Words, *T78–T79, T93, T109* **Word Wall**, *T62, T72, T82, T96, T104*	✓ Comprehension: Inferences: Drawing Conclusions, *T64, T74, T86, T87, T88, T98, T106* **Strategies: Predict/Infer,** *T64, T74, T85, T86, T98* **Phonics/Decoding,** *T93*
WEEK 3 **Read Aloud** **The Amazing Little Porridge Pot** **Big Books** **Tortillas and Lullabies** **Shoes From Grandpa** **Social Studies Links** **Families** **Which Would You Choose?** **Phonics Library** *"Cat's Surprise"* 	✓ Phonemic Awareness: Beginning Sounds, *T119, T129, T139, T147, T155* ✓ Initial Consonant *n, T124–T125, T132–T133* ✓ Review Initial Consonant *n, T142, T150–T151* Phonics Review: Familiar Consonants; *b, m, n, r, s, t, T125, T132, T144, T152, T158, T160*	High-Frequency Words, *T134–T135, T143, T159* Word Wall, *T118, T128, T138, T146, T154*	✓ Comprehension: Inferences: Drawing Conclusions, *T120, T140, T141, T148, T149, T156* ✓ Story Structure: Character/Setting, *T130, T156* **Strategies: Summarize,** *T120, T130, T140* Evaluate, *T131, T148* **Phonics/Decoding,** *T143*

<table>
<tr><td>

Pacing

- This theme is designed to take approximately 3 weeks, depending on your students' needs.

</td><td>

Multi–age Classroom

Related theme—

- **Grade 1:** *Family and Friends*

</td><td>

Technology

Education Place: www.eduplace.com Log on to Education Place for more activities relating to *We're a Family*.

Lesson Planner CD-ROM: Customize your planning for *We're a Family* with the Lesson Planner.

</td></tr>
</table>

Word Work		Writing & Language			Centers
High-Frequency Word Practice	**Exploring Words**	**Oral Language**	**Writing**	**Listening/ Speaking/Viewing**	**Content Areas**
Matching Words, *T14* Building Sentences, *T24*	Family Words, *T38, T46, T54*	**Using Movement Words** • create a chart, *T15* **Vocabulary Expansion** • using family words, *T25*	**Shared Writing** • recording observations, *T39* **Interactive Writing** • writing a journal entry, *T47* **Independent Writing** • Journals, *T55*	Viewing and Speaking, *T15* Listening and Speaking, *T25*	Book Center, *T11, T35* Phonics Center, *T13, T21, T45* Writing Center, *T25* Art Center, *T19, T35*
Matching Words, *T70* Building Sentences, *T80*	Family Words, *T94, T102, T110*	**Using Exact Naming Words** • naming words chart, *T71* **Vocabulary Expansion** • types of clothing, *T81*	**Shared Writing** • writing a grocery list, *T95* **Interactive Writing** • choosing a good title, *T103* **Independent Writing** • Journals, *T111*	Viewing and Speaking, *T71, T81* Listening and Speaking, *T95* Speaking, *T103*	Book Center, *T65* Phonics Center, *T69, T77, T101* Writing Center, *T71* Math Center, *T75, T91* Art Center, *T81, T91* Dramatic Play Center, *T65, T103*
Matching Words, *T126* Building Sentences, *T136*	Environmental Print, *T144, T152, T160*	**Using Action Words** • naming action words, *T127* **Vocabulary Expansion** • using order words, *T137*	**Shared Writing** • using order words, *T145* **Interactive Writing** • using order words, *T153* **Independent Writing** • Journals, *T161*	Viewing and Speaking, *T137* Listening and Speaking, *T145* Speaking, *T153*	Book Center, *T121* Phonics Center, *T125, T133, T151* Writing Center, *T127* Dramatic Play Center, *T121* Art Center, *T131, T141, T149* Math Center, *T137*

Planning for Assessment

Use these resources to meet your assessment needs. For additional information, see the *Teacher's Assessment Handbook.*

Emerging Literacy Survey

Diagnostic Planning

Emerging Literacy Survey

- If you have used this survey to obtain baseline data on the skills children brought with them to kindergarten, this might be a good time to re-administer all or parts of the survey to chart progress, to identify areas of strength and need, and to test the need for early intervention.

Ongoing Assessment

Phonemic Awareness:

- **Practice Book,** pp. 75–76, 85–86, 95–96

Phonics:

- **Practice Book,** pp. 77, 80, 87, 90, 100–101

Comprehension:

- Reading Responses in **Practice Book**, pp. 73–74, 79, 83–84, 89, 93–94, 97

Writing:

- Writing samples for portfolios

Informal Assessment:

- **Diagnostic Checks**, pp. T23, T34, T45, T53, T79, T90, T101, T109, T135, T151, T159

Theme Skills Test

End-of-Theme Assessment

Theme Skills Test:

- Assesses children's mastery of specific reading and language arts skills taught in the theme.

Kindergarten Benchmarks

For your planning, listed here are the instructional goals and activities that help develop benchmark behaviors for kindergartners. Use this list to plan instruction and to monitor children's progress. See the Checklist of skills found on T163.

Theme Lessons and Activities:	Benchmark Behaviors:
Oral Language • songs, rhymes, chants, finger plays • shared reading	• can listen to a story attentively • can participate in the shared reading experience
Phonemic Awareness • beginning sounds	• can blend sounds into meaningful units
Phonics • initial consonants *t, b, n*	• can name single letters and their sounds • can decode some common CVC words
Concepts of Print • capital at the beginning of sentence • end punctuation (period, question mark) • directionality: return sweep	• can recognize common print conventions
Reading • wordless stories • high-frequency words *my, like*	• can read and write a few words • can select a letter to represent a sound
Comprehension • story structure: character/setting • inferences: drawing conclusions	• can think critically about a text • can use effective reading strategies
Writing and Language • drawing and labeling images • using naming words	• can label pictures using phonetic spellings • can write independently

Launching the Theme

We're a Family

Theme Poster: We're a Family

▶ **Using the Theme Poster**

Display the Theme Poster and read the title. Explain that in this theme children will learn more about families. ***Who do you think the people are in these pictures?*** Hang up the poster, so that children can refer to it throughout the theme.

- **Week 1** After reading *Tortillas and Lullabies,* have children describe the people in a family pictured on the poster. Have them share their special family traditions.
- **Week 2** As a follow up to *Shoes from Grandpa,* have small groups talk about grandparents or older friends who are special to them.
- **Week 3** After rereading *Families* and *Which Would You Choose?,* talk about how the families in the poster are playing and working together. Then have children tell about how their own families play and work together.

Multi-age Classroom

Related theme:

Grade 1 . . . Family and Friends

Grade K . . . We're a Family

▶ Theme Poem: "Little Arabella Stiller"

Look at the illustration of the poem together, and ask children to describe what they see. Elicit descriptive language for the caterpillar such as *furry, soft, wiggly.* Read the poem aloud. Ask children what they think the poet meant by calling the caterpillar a *wooly caterpillar.*

Little Arabella Stiller

Little Arabella Stiller
Found a wooly caterpillar.
First it crawled up on her mother,
Then up on her baby brother.
All said, "Arabella Stiller,
Take away that caterpillar."

a Traditional Rhyme

14

Higglety Pigglety: A Book of Rhymes, page 14

On-Going Project

Materials • Blackline Master 48 • crayons • markers • snack food

Family Breakfast Tell children that toward the end of this theme, you will celebrate with a breakfast gathering. Have children use **Blackline Master 48** to write their invitations. Family members or caregivers can join the class to celebrate what the children have learned during the them. Children can:

• Sing the Alphafriend songs.
• Serve simple snacks.
• Share their family drawings.
• Share a favorite Big Book from the theme.

Dear Mom and Dad
Please come to our Family Breakfast.
When Thursday, November 27
Time 8:30–9:30
                              Love,
                                Aki

Technology

www.eduplace.com
Log onto *Education Place* for more activities relating to *We're a Family.*

Lesson Planner CD-ROM
Customize your planning for *We're a Family* with the Lesson Planner.

Book Adventure
www.bookadventure.org
This Internet reading-incentive program provides thousands of titles for students to read.

Home Connection

Send home the theme newsletter for *We're a Family* to introduce the theme and suggest home activities (**Blackline Master 43**).

For other suggestions relating to *We're a Family,* see **Home/Community Connections.**

Classroom Routines

We're a Family

To introduce a routine...

1. Demonstrate the routine for the class.
2. Cycle every child through the routine at least once with supervision.
3. Establish ground rules for acceptable work products.
4. Check children's work.
5. Praise children's growing independence.

Teacher's Note

If some children do not circulate to all the centers on their own, you can help them select a different center prior to the beginning of your Group Time.

Instructional Routines

What's the Sound?

During the Daily Phonemic Awareness activity, say two words that begin with the same sound. After you say the words, have children say the words. Then help them isolate and name the beginning sound. You can also play What's the Sound? by saying just one word, and having the children identify the beginning sound.

Name That Word

When playing Name That Word, say two words. Have children repeat the words. Then ask them, for example, which word begins with Tiggy Tiger's sound, /t/. Confirm the children's responses. **Yes, ten *begins with* /t/.**

Management Routines

Center Sign Up

Do too many children want to work at the same center during your Group Time? You can remedy this situation, if you limit the number of spots at each center. First make oaktag name tags with self-stick dots attached to the back of each. Center signs have receiving self-stick dots. When children sign up to work in an area, they place their name tag on the center sign. If there are no empty spaces on the sign, the center is closed. When a child leaves a center, another child may come to work there. Initially, you may need to remind children to take their name tags when they leave to go work in another center.

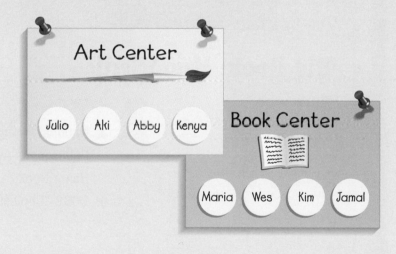

Literature for Week 1
Different texts for different purposes

Teacher Read Aloud

Jonathan and His Mommy
by Irene Smalls Illustrated by Michael Hays

Purposes
- oral language
- listening strategy
- comprehension skill

Awards
- ★ Best Books for Children
- ★ American Bookseller "Pick of the Lists"
- ★ Horn Book Recommended Paperback

Big Books:

Higglety Pigglety: A Book of Rhymes

Purposes
- oral language development
- phonemic awareness

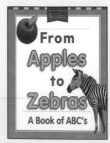

From Apples to Zebras: A Book of ABC's

Purposes
- alphabet recognition
- letters and sounds

Tortillas and Lullabies
Tortillas y cancioncitas

BY LYNN REISER
PICTURES BY "CORAZONES VALIENTES"

Big Book: Main Selection

Purposes
- concepts of print
- reading strategy
- story language
- comprehension skills

Awards
- ★ National Parenting Publications Award Honor Book
- ★ CCBC "Choices"

Also available in Little Big Book and audiotape

Leveled Books

On My Way Paperback

Nicky Takes a Bath
by **Sam Fonte**
Page T157

Little Readers for Guided Reading
Collection K

Houghton Mifflin Classroom Bookshelf
Level K

Technology

www.eduplace.com
Log on to *Education Place* for more activities relating to *We're a Family*.

www.bookadventure.org
This free Internet reading incentive program provides thousands of titles for students to read.

HOUGHTON MIFFLIN
Reading

Tortillas and Lullabies
Tortillas y cancioncitas

BY **LYNN REISER**
PICTURES BY **'CORAZONES VALIENTES'**

Includes:
Social Studies Link

Also in the Big Book:
– Social Studies Link

Purposes:

- reading strategies
- comprehension skills
- concepts of print

Phonics Library

HOUGHTON MIFFLIN
Reading

Phonics Library

Colors All Around

Also available in Take-Home version

Purpose

- applying phonics skills and high-frequency words

Instructional Goals

Learning to Read

- ✓ *Phonemic Awareness:* Beginning Sounds

Strategy Focus: Evaluate

- ✓ *Comprehension Skill:* Story Structure: Characters/Setting

- ✓ *Phonics Skills*

Phonemic Awareness: Beginning Sound /t/

Initial Consonant *T, t*

Compare and Review: s

- ✓ *High-Frequency Word: my*

- ✓ *Concepts of Print:* Return Sweep; Capitalize First Word in Sentence; End Punctuation

Word Work

High-Frequency Word Practice: Family Words

Writing & Language

Vocabulary Skills: Using Movement Words, Using Family Words

Writing Skills: Recording Observations, Writing a Journal Entry

✓ = tested skills

Leveled Books

Have children read in appropriate levels daily.

Phonics Library
On My Way Practice Readers
Little Big Books
Houghton Mifflin Classroom Bookshelf

Day 1

Opening Routines, *T8–T9*

【Word / Wall】

- Phonemic Awareness: Beginning Sounds

Teacher Read Aloud
Jonathan and His Mommy, T10–T11
- **Strategy:** Evaluate
- **Comprehension:** Story Structure: Characters/Setting

Phonics
Instruction
- Phonemic Awareness, Beginning Sound /t/, *T12–T13; Practice Book, 75–76*

High-Frequency Word Practice
- Words: *I, my, see, T14*

Oral Language
- Using Movement Words, *T15*
- Viewing and Speaking, *T15*

Managing Small Groups
Teacher-Led Group
- Reread familiar **Phonics Library** selections

Independent Groups
- Finish *Practice Book, 73–76*
- *Phonics Center:* Theme 3, Week 1, Day 1
- Book, other Centers

Day 2

Opening Routines, *T16–T17*

【Word / Wall】

- Phonemic Awareness: Beginning Sounds

Sharing the Big Book
Tortillas and Lullabies, T18–T19
- **Strategy:** Evaluate
- **Comprehension:** Story Structure: Characters/Setting

Phonics
Instruction, Practice
- Initial Consonant *t, T20–T21*
- *Practice Book, 77*

High-Frequency Word
- New Word: *my, T22–T23*
- *Practice Book, 78*

High-Frequency Word Practice
- Building Sentences, *T24*

Vocabulary Expansion
- Using Family Words, *T25*
- Listening and Speaking, *T25*

Managing Small Groups
Teacher-Led Group
- Begin *Practice Book, 77–78* and handwriting **Blackline Masters 176 or 202.**

Independent Groups
- Finish *Practice Book, 77–78* and handwriting **Blackline Masters 176 or 202.**
- *Phonics Center:* Theme 3, Week 1, Day 2
- Art, Writing, other Centers

Technology

Lesson Planner CD-ROM: Customize your planning for *We're Family* with the Lesson Planner.

Day 3

Opening Routines, *T26–T27*

Word Wall
- **Phonemic Awareness:** Beginning Sounds

Sharing the Big Book
Tortillas and Lullabies, T28–T33
- **Strategy:** Evaluate
- **Comprehension:** Story Structure: Characters/Setting, *T29; Practice Book, 79*
- **Concepts of Print:** Return Sweep; Capitalize First Word in Sentence; End Punctuation, *T30–T31*

Phonics
Practice, Application
- Consonant *t, T36–T37*

Instruction
- Beginning Letter *t, T36–T37*
- **Phonics Library:** "The Birthday Party," *T37*

Exploring Words
- Family Words, *T38*

✎ **Shared Writing**
- Recording Observations, *T39*

Managing Small Groups
Teacher-Led Group
- Read **Phonics Library** selection "The Birthday Party"
- Begin *Practice Book, 79*

Independent Groups
- Finish *Practice Book, 79*
- Art, Book, other Centers

Day 4

Opening Routines, *T40–T41*

Word Wall
- **Phonemic Awareness:** Beginning Sounds

Sharing the Big Book
Social Studies Link: "Families," *T42–T43*
- **Strategy:** Evaluate
- **Comprehension:** Story Structure: Characters/Setting
- **Concepts of Print:** Capitalize First Word in Sentence; End Punctuation; Return Sweep

Phonics
Practice
- Review Initial Consonant *t, T44–T45; Practice Book, 80*

Exploring Words
- Family Words, *T46*

✎ **Interactive Writing**
- Writing a Journal Entry, *T47*

Managing Small Groups
Teacher-Led Group
- Reread **Phonics Library** selection "The Birthday Party"
- Begin *Practice Book, 80*

Independent Groups
- Finish *Practice Book, 80*
- *Phonics Center:* Theme 3, Week 1, Day 4

Day 5

Opening Routines, *T48–T49*

Word Wall
- **Phonemic Awareness:** Beginning Sounds

Revisiting the Literature
Comprehension: Story Structures: Character/Setting, *T50*
Building Fluency
- **Phonics Library:** "The Birthday Party," *T51*

Phonics
Review
- Initial Consonant *m, s, t, T52*

High-Frequency Word Review
- Words: *I, see, my, T53; Practice Book, 81*

Exploring Words
- Family Words, *T54*

✎ **Independent Writing**
- Journals: Favorite Family Activity, *T55*

Managing Small Groups
Teacher-Led Group
- Reread familiar **Phonics Library** selections
- Begin *Practice Book, 81,* **Blackline Master 36.**

Independent Groups
- Reread **Phonics Library** selections
- Finish *Practice Book, 81,* **Blackline Master 36.**
- Centers

Setting up the Centers

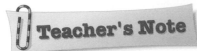

Ask families to send in magazines to use in the Art Center.

Phonics Center

Materials • Phonics Center materials for Theme 3, Week 1

Pairs work together to sort Picture Cards by initial sound. Cut the letter grids apart and put them into plastic bags, according to color. Put out the Workmats and open the Direction Chart to the appropriate day. See pages T13, T21, and T45 for this week's Phonics Center activities.

Book Center

Materials • picture books about families

Children can talk about families as they browse through picture books. Feature contemporary and classic stories such as *Katy No Pocket* by Emmy Payne, *Big Brother, Little Brother* by Penny Dale, and *Little Bear's Visit* by Else Holmelund Minarik. See pages T11 and T35 for this week's Book Center activities.

Writing Center

> **Materials** • drawing paper • markers

Children draw family pictures. They can refer to the chart made on Day 2 to help them label their pictures. See page T25 for this week's Writing Center activity.

Art Center

> **Materials** • magazines • drawing paper • crayons and markers

Children find and discuss pictures of family activities. They also draw pictures of favorite activities to do with a family member. See pages T19 and T35 for this week's Art Center activities.

Learning to Read

Day 1

Day at a Glance

Learning to Read

Read Aloud:

Jonathan and His Mommy

☑ **Learning About /t/**, page T12

Word Work

☑ **High-Frequency Word Practice,** page T14

Writing & Language

Oral Language, *page T15*

 Half-Day Kindergarten

☑ Indicates lessons for tested skills. Choose additional activities as time allows.

Opening

Calendar

Sunday	Monday	Tuesday	Wednesday	Thursday	Friday	Saturday
			1	2	3	4
5	6	7	8	9	10	11
12	13	14	15	16	17	18
19	20	21	22	23	24	25
26	27	28	29	30	31	

Have children repeat the names of the days of the week after you as you track the print. Point to the Saturday and Sunday that have just passed. Ask: *What did your family do over the weekend?*

Daily Message

Modeled Writing Celebrate starting a new reading theme by including the theme title in your daily message.

Today we start a new theme called We're a Family. Who is in your family?

Have children chant the spelling of each word on the Word Wall today: **I** *spells* **I** *and* **s-e-e** *spells* **see.** Ask children to use the words in oral sentences.

✓ Daily Phonemic Awareness
Beginning Sounds

- *Listen as I say two words:* ten, top. *Say the words with me listening for the beginning sounds:* ten, top. *Do you hear the same sound at the beginning of each word? So do I.* Ten *and* top *both begin with* /t/.

- Tell children that they will now play Same Sound Sort. Explain that you will say two words. If the words begin with the same sound, they should raise their hands. If the words do not begin with the same sound, they should cover their ears.

down/dog	boy/girl	corn/cat
juice/cup	rice/rain	hop/hen
song/sack	new/nice	laugh/cry

Getting Ready to Learn

To help plan their day, tell children that they will

- listen to a story called *Jonathan and His Mommy.*

- meet a new Alphafriend, Tiggy Tiger.

- explore more about families in the Book Center.

Day 1

HOUGHTON MIFFLIN
Reading

Jonathan and His Mommy
by Irene Smalls Illustrated by Michael Hays

Purposes • oral language • listening strategy
• comprehension skill

Selection Summary
Jonathan likes walking and talking with his mother. While taking a walk, they move in different ways. Finally, when they are tired, they Jonathan-step and Mommy-step all the way back home.

Key Concepts
Different ways of walking
City neighborhoods

MEETING INDIVIDUAL NEEDS

English Language Learners

Before reading, demonstrate the different ways of walking mentioned in the story. Then have children follow your lead. For example, say and act out: *Take big giant steps.* Do this as a game, changing directions often and fast.

Teacher Read Aloud
Oral Language/Comprehension

▶ Building Background

Ask children to remember walks they have taken. *Where did you go? What did you see? Who went with you?* Then introduce the book *Jonathan and His Mommy.* Read aloud the title and the names of the author and illustrator. Tell children that this book is about a walk, too.

Strategy: Evaluate

Teacher Modeling Tell children that good readers think about the way a book makes them feel. Model the strategy to evaluate a book.

> **Think Aloud**
>
> *As I read, I will think about the way the story makes me feel. When I look at the cover, it looks like Jonathan and his mother look like people who like to have fun. I like to have fun, too.*
>
> *As I read, I'll ask myself questions about the story to see if I like it and why.*

✓ Comprehension Focus:
Story Structure: Characters/Setting

Teacher Modeling Explain to children that good readers pay attention to important story parts to help them understand a story better.

>
> **Think Aloud**
>
> *One important story part is the characters or who the story is about. In this story, Jonathan and his mother are the main characters. Another important story part is the setting, or where the story takes place. The pictures tell me that Jonathan and his mother live in a city neighborhood. I see apartment buildings, sidewalks, streets, stores, a playground, and a park.*

▶ Listening to the Story

Read the story with expression, changing your voice as Jonathan and his mother change their way of moving.

▶ Responding

Summarizing the Story *Help children summarize parts of the story.*

■ *Who are the main characters in the story? Where does the story take place?*

■ *What did Jonathan and his mother do in the story? What kind of steps did they take?*

■ *Why do you think Jonathan likes to go walking and talking with his mother? Would you like to walk and talk like this? Why or why not?*

■ *What was your favorite part of the story? How did this book make you feel?*

Practice Book pages 73–74 Children will complete the pages during small group time.

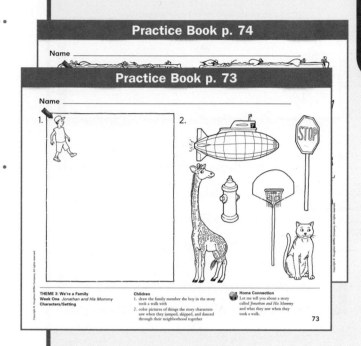

At Group Time

Book Center

Feature stories about all kinds of families in the Book Center. Be sure to include a mix of classic and contemporary stories. *Katy No-Pocket* by Emmy Payne, *Big Brother, Little Brother* by Penny Dale, and *When Will Sarah Come?* by Elizabeth Fitzgerald Howard are good choices, along with *Peter's Chair* by Ezra Jack Keats, *A Birthday Basket for Tía* by Pat Mora, and *Little Bear's Visit* by Else Holmelund Minarik.

OBJECTIVES
◎

Children

- identify pictures whose names begin with /t/

MATERIALS

- **Alphafriend Cards** *Sammy Seal, Tiggy Tiger*
- **Alphafriend Audiotape** *Theme 3*
- **Alphafolder** *Tiggy Tiger*
- **Picture Cards** *sandbox, six, sun, tent, tooth, top*
- **Phonics Center:** Theme 3, Week 1, Day 1

Home Connection

A take-home version of Tiggy Tiger's song is an **Alphafriends Blackline Master.** Children can share the song with their families.

Phonemic Awareness
✅ Beginning Sound

▶ Introducing the Alphafriend: Tiggy Tiger

Tell children that today they will meet a new Alphafriend. Recall with children that Alphafriends help them to remember the sounds for the letters of the alphabet. Have children listen as you share a riddle to help them guess who their new Alphafriend is.

1 Alphafriend Riddle Read these clues:

- *Our Alphafriend's sound is /t/. Say it with me: /t/.*

- *This animal is a kind of wild cat that lives in the jungle.*

- *This cat purrs, but it also growls—so watch out!*

- *He has orange and black stripes on his fur and sharp claws.*

When most hands are up, call on children until they guess *tiger*.

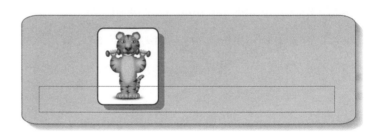

2 Pocket Chart Display Tiggy Tiger in a pocket chart. Say his name, stretching the /t/ sound slightly, and have children echo this.

3 📼 **Alphafriend Audiotape**
Play Tiggy Tiger's song. *Listen for /t/ words in Tiggy's song.*

4 Alphafolder Have children look at the scene and name all the /t/ pictures.

5 Summarize

- *What is our Alphafriend's name? What is his sound?*

- *What words in our Alphafriend's song start with /t/?*

- *Each time you look at Tiggy Tiger this week, remember the /t/ sound.*

Tiggy Tiger's Song
(Tune: "Twinkle, Twinkle Little Star")

Tiggy Tiger can tickle his toes.
Tiggy Tiger can tap his nose.
Tiggy Tiger can turn around.
Tiggy Tiger can touch the ground.
Tiggy Tiger can tie his shoes.
Tiggy Tiger can count by twos.

▶ Listening for /t/

Compare and Review: /s/ Display Alphafriend *Sammy Seal* opposite *Tiggy Tiger.* Review each character's sound.

Tell children you'll hold up and name some Picture Cards and they should signal "thumbs up" for each one that begins like Tiggy's name. Volunteers put the cards below Tiggy's picture. For "thumbs down" words, volunteers put the cards below Sammy Seal.

Pictures: *tent, sandbox, tooth, six, top, sun*

Tell children they will sort more pictures in the Phonics Center today.

▶ Apply

Practice Book pages 75–76 Children will complete the pages at small group time.

At Group Time

Phonics Center

Use the Phonics Center Materials for **Theme 3, Week 1, Day 1**.

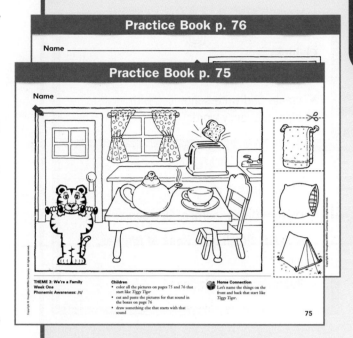

Name _____

THEME 3: We're a Family
Week One
Phonemic Awareness: /t/

Children
• color all the pictures on pages 75 and 76 that start like *Tiggy Tiger*
• cut and paste the pictures for that sound in the boxes on page 76
• draw something else that starts with that sound

Home Connection Let's name the things on the front and back that start like *Tiggy Tiger.*

75

Word Work

Day 1

OBJECTIVES

Children

- read high-frequency words
- create and write sentences with high-frequency words

MATERIALS

- **Word Cards** *I, my, see*
- **Picture Cards** *berries, feet, sandals, toys*
- ***Higglety Pigglety: A Book of Rhymes,*** page 44
- **Punctuation Card:** period

High-Frequency Word Practice

▶ Matching Words

- Display Word Cards for the high-frequency words *I* and *see* in a pocket chart. Call on children to identify each word and to match it on the Word Wall.

- *I'll read a poem. You listen to hear if these words are used in it.*

- Read the poem "Rhyme" on page 44 of *Higglety Pigglety.* **Did you hear any of these words in the poem? Let's see which Word Cards you can match to the words in the poem.**

Higglety Pigglety: A Book of Rhymes, page 44

Writing Opportunity Place the Word Cards *I* and *see* in a pocket chart as a sentence stem. Have children read the words with you. Then display assorted Picture Cards and ask children to use them to complete the sentence. Children may then write and illustrate one of the sentences or use the words to create their own sentences with rebus pictures.

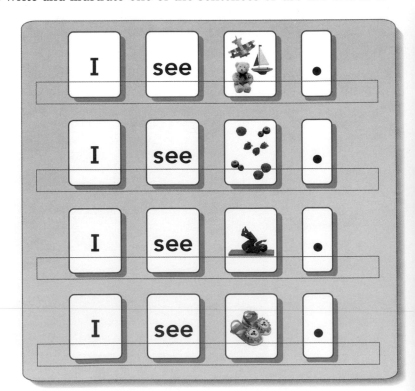

Oral Language

▶ Using Movement Words

Viewing and Speaking Display *Jonathan and His Mommy.* Ask children to recall the ways Jonathan and his mother moved while on their walk. Create a chart to list these ways. Page through the book to help children remember the ways Jonathan and his mommy moved.

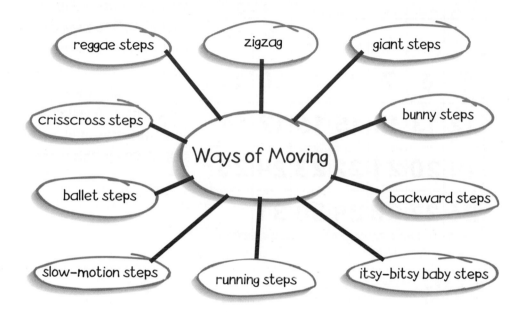

reggae steps

zigzag

giant steps

crisscross steps

bunny steps

Ways of Moving

ballet steps

backward steps

slow-motion steps

running steps

itsy-bitsy baby steps

Using the chart as a guide, have a small group of children secretly select a way of walking. As they act out the movement, the rest of the class guesses what the movement is. Continue with other small groups.

OBJECTIVES

Children
- list ways of walking
- act out ways of walking

MATERIALS

- **Read Aloud:** *Jonathan and His Mommy*

English Language Learners

When listing ways of walking, draw stick figures or find magazine pictures that show the action. Display the pictures next to the words so that English language learners have a visual reference.

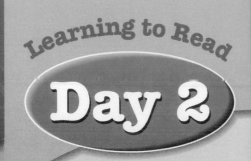

Day 2

Day at a Glance

Learning to Read

Big Book:

Tortillas and Lullabies

✓ **Phonics: Initial Consonant *t*,** page T22

✓ **High-Frequency Word:** *my*, page T21

Word Work

High-Frequency Word Practice, page T24

Writing & Language

Vocabulary Expansion, page T25

 Half-Day Kindergarten

✓ Indicates lessons for tested skills. Choose additional activities as time allows.

Opening

Calendar

Sunday	Monday	Tuesday	Wednesday	Thursday	Friday	Saturday
			1	2	3	4
5	6	7	8	9	10	11
12	13	14	15	16	17	18
19	20	21	22	23	24	25
26	27	28	29	30	31	

Review the days of the month that have occurred so far. Count how many days are in the month. *On what day of the week did the month begin? On what day will the month end?* Help children find these days on the calendar. Together, count the days until a special date in this month.

Daily Message

Modeled Writing As you write, have children provide the initial consonants for known sounds: *The first word I want to write is Sasha. What is the beginning sound in Sasha? What letter do I write to spell this sound?* Point out that the first word in a sentence always begins with a capital letter.

Sasha's mom will read to us.

Distribute Word Cards for the words on the Word Wall. Have children match the cards to the words on the Word Wall. Have children chant the spelling of each word. Repeat, distributing the words to different volunteers.

Routines

 ## Daily Phonemic Awareness
Beginning Sounds

- Read "I Went Upstairs" on page 12 of *Higglety Pigglety.*

- Tell children that they will play What's the Sound? *I will say a word from the poem. You listen for the beginning sound and tell me the sound your hear. Now listen:* bed.

- When most hands are up, have children voice the sound. *Yes,/b/is the sound at the beginning of* bed.

- Continue in a similar manner with other words from the poem: *make, head, milk, cow, bake, sow, pie.*

I Went Upstairs

I went upstairs to make my bed.
I made a mistake and bumped my head.
I went downstairs to milk my cow.
I made a mistake and milked the sow.
I went to the kitchen to bake a pie.
I made a mistake and baked a fly.

a Jump-Rope Rhyme

12

Higglety Pigglety: A Book of Rhymes, **page 12**

Getting Ready to Learn

To help plan their day, tell children that they will

- listen to a Big Book: *Tortillas and Lullabies.*

- learn the new letters, *T* and *t,* and see words that begin with *t.*

- draw and label family pictures in the Art Center.

Big Book

HOUGHTON MIFFLIN
Reading

Tortillas and Lullabies
Tortillas y cancioncitas

BY **LYNN REISER**
PICTURES BY **'CORAZONES VALIENTES'**

Includes Social Studies Link

Purposes • concepts of print • story language
• reading strategy

Selection Summary

A young girl views how four generations of her family have made tortillas, gathered flowers, washed dresses, and sung lullabies, observing that each time the way was similar yet different.

Key Concepts

Family relationships
Family traditions

MEETING INDIVIDUAL NEEDS

English Language Learners

Introduce vocabulary that names family members. If possible, have children bring pictures of their families and have them name the people in the pictures. Discuss also traditional or cultural food children eat at home. Some English language learners may not be familiar with tortillas. If possible, have some available for children to try.

Sharing the Big Book
Oral Language/Comprehension

▶ Building Background

Ask children to remember favorite things they have done with family members. Talk about activities they may have done with a parent and also with a grandparent. Then introduce the book *Tortillas and Lullabies.* Tell children that this book is about families, too.

Strategy: Evaluate

Teacher Modeling Remind children that good readers think about how a story makes them feel. Model the Evaluate Strategy as you display pages 4 and 5.

Think Aloud

When I read a story, I think about why I like the story or why I don't like the story. I think about how the story makes me feel.

This picture shows the great-grandmother making tortillas for her daughter. The next one shows the grandmother making tortillas for her daughter. I know I like it when my grandmother or mom cooks for me. It makes me feel happy. I think I like this story because the moms are doing things for the daughters.

✓ Comprehension Focus:
Story Structure: Characters/Setting

Teacher Modeling Remind children that good readers think about the story characters and the setting.

Think Aloud

I know that the characters in this story are the great-grandmother, the grandmother, the mother, and the girl. When I look at the pictures, it looks like the characters are at their homes. As I read, I'll think about how the characters and the settings are alike and different.

▶ Sharing the Story

Read the selection aloud, tracking the print with a pointer or your hand. Pause to help children identify the story characters and comment on the illustrations. Point out the Spanish words on each page. Tell children that these words say the same things as the English words.

▶ Responding

Personal Response Encourage children to use the language of the story as they react to it.

■ *Who are the characters in the story?*

■ *How is what each character does the same? How is it different?*

■ *What do you like most that your mother or father does for you? Did your grandparents do any of these things for your parents?*

■ *Which story part did you like best? Why?*

At Group Time

Art Center

Materials • old magazines • drawing paper • crayons

Have children find and cut out from magazines pictures of family members doing things together. Have children paste their pictures onto drawing paper. Allow time for children to share their pictures with the class and to speculate about the family relationships pictured.

MEETING INDIVIDUAL NEEDS

Extra Support

Some children may have trouble understanding the mother-daughter relationships on each page and the generation relationships to the storyteller. Go through the book page by page helping children to identify first the mother and daughter in each picture, and then explaining the generation relationship to the storyteller.

Learning to Read
Day 2

Phonics

✓ Initial Consonant t

▶ Develop Phonemic Awareness

Beginning Sound Read the lyrics to Tiggy Tiger's song and have children echo it line-for-line. Have them listen for /t/ words and "tap" the floor each time they hear one.

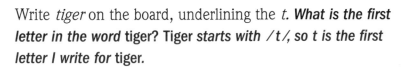

> **Tiggy Tiger's Song**
> (Tune: "Twinkle, Twinkle Little Star")
>
> Tiggy Tiger can tickle his toes.
> Tiggy Tiger can tap his nose.
> Tiggy Tiger can turn around.
> Tiggy Tiger can touch the ground.
> Tiggy Tiger can tie his shoes.
> Tiggy Tiger can count by twos.

▶ Connect Sounds to Letters

Beginning Letter Display the *Tiggy Tiger* card, and have children name the letter on the picture. Say: *The letter* t *stands for the sound /t/, as in tiger. When you see a t, remember Tiggy Tiger. That will help you remember the sound /t/.*

Write *tiger* on the board, underlining the *t*. *What is the first letter in the word* tiger? Tiger *starts with /t/, so t is the first letter I write for* tiger.

Compare and Review: s In a pocket chart, display the *Tiggy Tiger* card along with the Letter Cards *t* and *s*. Place the Picture Cards in random order. Review the sound for *s*. In turn, children name a picture, say the beginning sound, and put the card below the right letter.

Tell children they will sort more pictures at the Phonics Center today.

OBJECTIVES ◎

Children

- identify words that begin with /t/
- identify pictures whose names start with the letter *t*
- form the letters *Tt*

MATERIALS

- **Alphafriend Card** *Tiggy Tiger*
- **Letter Cards** *s, t*
- **Picture Cards** *sandwich, seal, six, ten, tooth, top*
- **Blackline Master 176**
- **Phonics Center:** Theme 3, Week 1, Day 2

MEETING INDIVIDUAL NEEDS

Extra Support

To help children remember the sound for *t*, point out that the letter's name gives a clue to its sound: *t*, /t/.

▶ Handwriting

Writing *T, t* Tell children that now they'll learn to write the letters that stand for / t /: capital *T* and small *t*. Write each letter as you recite the handwriting rhyme. Children can chant each rhyme as they "write" the letter in the air.

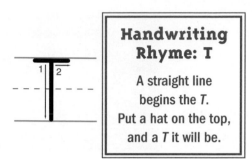

Handwriting Rhyme: T
A straight line begins the *T*. Put a hat on the top, and a *T* it will be.

Handwriting Rhyme: t
Not as tall, straight down for small *t*. Cross near the middle, a *t*, you'll see!

▶ Apply

Practice Book page 77 Children will complete this page at small group time.

Blackline Master 176 This page provides additional handwriting practice.

At Group Time

Phonics Center

Use the Phonics Center materials for **Theme 3, Week 1, Day 2**.

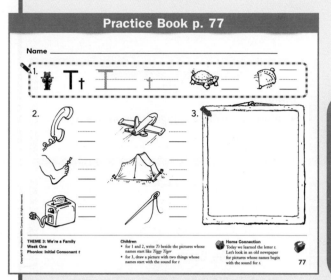

Practice Book p. 77

Name _____

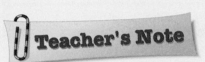

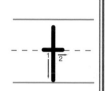

THEME 3: We're a Family
Week One
Phonics: Initial Consonant *t*

Children
• for 1 and 2, write *Tt* beside the pictures whose names start like *Tiggy Tiger*
• for 3, draw a picture with two things whose names start with the sound for *t*

Home Connection
Today we learned the letter *t*. Let's look in an old newspaper for pictures whose names begin with the sound for *t*.

77

🖇 Teacher's Note

Handwriting practice for the continuous stroke style is available on **Blackline Master 202.**

Portfolio Opportunity

Save the Practice Book page to show children's grasp of the letter-sound association for *t*.

DAY 2

Phonics (T21)

OBJECTIVES

Children

• read and write the high-frequency word *my*

MATERIALS

• **Word Cards** *I, my, see*

• **Picture Cards** *bike, cat, dog, doll*

• **Punctuation Card:** period

• ***Higglety Pigglety: A Book of Rhymes,*** page 7

✔ High-Frequency Word

New Word: my

▶ Teach

Tell children that they will learn to read and write *my*, a word they will often see in stories. Say *my* and use it in context.

> *My* shirt is blue.
> This is *my* book.
> Are you *my* friend?

Write *my* on the board, and have children spell it as you point to each letter. **Spell *my* with me,** m-y. Then lead children in a chant, clapping on each beat, to help them remember that *my* is spelled *m-y*: **m-y, my! m-y, my.**

Word Wall Ask children to help you decide where *my* should be posted. As needed, prompt children by pointing out that *my* begins with the letter *m*. When children find the letter *m* on the Word Wall, add *my* beneath it. Remind children to look there when they need to remember how to write the word

▶ Practice

Reading Build the following sentences in a pocket chart. Have children take turns reading the sentences aloud. Leave out the pocket chart so that children can practice building and reading sentences.

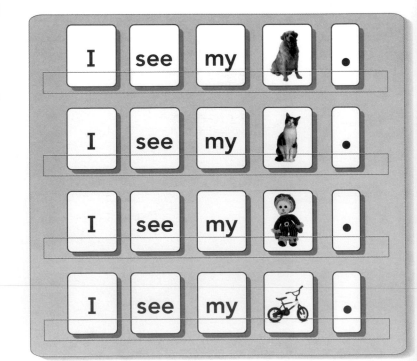

DAY 2

Display *Higglety Pigglety: A Book of Rhymes,* page 7.

■ Share the poem "Crackers and Crumbs" aloud.

■ Reread the poem, encouraging children to include the actions.

■ Read the poem a third time. *I'll read the poem one more time. This time I'll read slowly. You listen for the word* my. *If you hear it raise your hand.*

■ Call on children to point to the word *my* each time it appears in the poem.

Higglety Pigglety: A Book of Rhymes, page 7

▶ Apply

Practice Book page 78 Children will read and write *my* as they complete the Practice Book page.

Practice Book p. 78

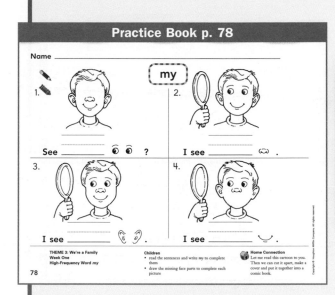

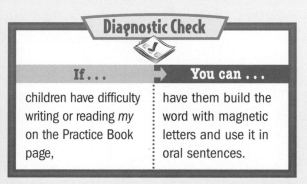

Diagnostic Check

If . . .	You can . . .
children have difficulty writing or reading *my* on the Practice Book page,	have them build the word with magnetic letters and use it in oral sentences.

High-Frequency Word **T23**

Teacher's Note

Some children may want to include color words when the describe what they see. Refer them to the Color Word Chart from Theme 2 or page 29 of *From Apples to Zebras: A Book of ABC's.*

High-Frequency Word Practice

▶ Building Sentences

Tell children that you want to build a sentence using the Word and Picture Cards.

■ Display the Word Cards in random order. Tell children that you will use these words to build your sentence. Review the words together. Then explain that you are ready to build the sentence.

■ *I want the first word to be* I. *Who can find that word?*

■ Continue building the sentence until you have the stem *I see my* _____.

■ Ask a volunteer to complete the sentence with one of the Picture Cards.

■ Read the completed sentence together, then continue with a new one.

Writing Opportunity Have children make an *I See* book, using the sentences in the pocket chart as a guide. Encourage them to show their books during Sharing Time.

Vocabulary Expansion

▶ Using Family Words

Remind children that in *Tortillas and Lullabies* they read about different women in one family. *Do you remember who the characters in this story were?*

Listening and Speaking List children's responses on chart paper. Be sure to include the Spanish words as well. Then explain that these are only a few of the people who might be in a family.

■ Brainstorm with children names for other family members.

■ As you list family member names on the chart, ask children if they have other names to describe these family members. Include them on the chart as well.

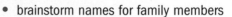

People in a Family

great-grandmother, bisabuela

grandmother, abuela   grandfather, abuela

mother, mamá   father, pápa, dad

daughter   son

                                   brother

At Group Time
Writing Center

Materials • drawing paper • markers

Have children draw pictures of their families. Children might draw a generation picture to show a grandparent, parent, and child. Children can also draw their nuclear family. Have children write or dictate labels for the people in their pictures.

Grandma   Mom   Dad   my brother   me

Day at a Glance

Learning to Read

Big Book:

Tortillas and Lullabies

☑ **Phonics:** Initial Consonant *t*, page T36

Word Work

Exploring Words, *page T38*

Writing & Language

Shared Writing, *page T39*

Half-Day Kindergarten

☑ Indicates lessons for tested skills. Choose additional activities as time allows.

Opening

Calendar

Sunday	Monday	Tuesday	Wednesday	Thursday	Friday	Saturday
			1	2	3	4
5	6	7	8	9	10	11
12	13	14	15	16	17	18
19	20	21	22	23	24	25
26	27	28	29	30	31	

For the duration of the theme, shift some of the "news from home" to the calendar routine. *Does your family have any special plans for the week? What are they? On what day will you and your family do this?*

Daily Message

Modeled Writing Incorporate children's names and a discussion of families into the daily message.

Maggie has a new puppy.

Tyrone has a picture of his baby sister.

Word Wall

Ask children if they can find the word that they added to the Word Wall yesterday. Choose a child to point to the word. Have children chant the spelling of the word: m-y *spells* my.

Daily Phonemic Awareness
Beginning Sounds

- *Let's listen for beginning sounds. I will say two words, you tell me which word begins with Tiggy Tiger's sound, /t/. Listen: ten, four.*

- *Say the words with me: ten, four. Which word begins with /t/?... Yes, ten begins with /t/.*

- Continue with the words shown.

toy/ball	teach/lion
free/toad	wheel/tall
short/tank	table/chair
fish/toe	bike/tooth
town/sing	

Getting Ready to Learn

To help plan their day, tell children that they will

- reread and talk about the Big Book: *Tortillas and Lullabies.*

- read a story called "The Birthday Party."

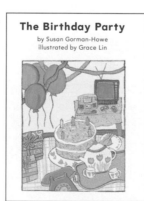

- draw pictures of family activity in the Art Center.

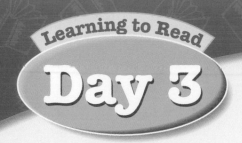
Sharing the Big Book

page 1

OBJECTIVES

Children

- identify characters and setting in a story
- recognize use of capital letter at the beginning of a sentence
- recognize use of end punctuation: period, question mark
- observe use of directionality: return sweep

pages 2–3

One
1
Uno

Tortillas

Tortillas

Big Book

Reading

Tortillas and Lullabies
Tortillas y cancioncitas

BY LYNN REISER
PICTURES BY 'CORAZONES VALIENTES'

Reading for Understanding Reread the story, noting the language pattern. Pause for Supporting Comprehension points.

MEETING INDIVIDUAL NEEDS

Extra Support

Point out details in the pictures to help children grasp the concept of past and present.

My great-grandmother made tortillas for my grandmother.

Mi bisabuela hacía tortillas para mi abuela.

My grandmother made tortillas for my mother.

Mi abuela hacía tortillas para mi mamá.

pages 4–5

My mother made tortillas for me,

and I made tortillas for my doll.

Mi mamá hacía tortillas para mí,

y yo hacía tortillas para mi muñeca.

pages 6–7

Every time it was the same, but different.

Cada vez era lo mismo, pero diferente.

pages 8–9

Two

Dos

2

Flowers

Flores

pages 10–11

▶ Supporting Comprehension

pages 4–5

Noting Details

■ *Who is the great-grandmother? What is she doing?* (The purple-haired woman is the great-grandmother; she is making tortillas.)

pages 4–7

Comprehension Focus: Story Structure: Characters/Setting

Teacher-Student Modeling Review that good readers note important story parts. *Who are the story characters?* (The characters are four women from the same family.) *What clues tell you where they live?* (The animals and plants help show a farm. I see a stove and a cabinet on page 6; they are in the kitchen. On page 7, the bed in the corner tells me that the girl is in her bedroom.)

pages 8–9

Strategy: Evaluate

Teacher-Student Modeling Recall that good readers have feelings about what they read. Prompts: *Do you agree with the girl? How are the tortillas cooked? Is it the same way, or is it different? How are they the same? How are they different?*

DAY 3

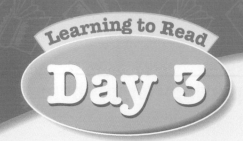

My grandmother gathered flowers
for my great-grandmother.

Mi abuela recogía flores
para mi bisabuela.

12

My mother gathered flowers
for my grandmother.

Mi mamá recogía flores
para mi abuela.

13

pages 12–13

▶ Supporting Comprehension

pages 12–15

Summarize

- *Where did each girl gather flowers for her mother?* (Grandmother gathered flowers from the forest; mother gathered wildflowers from the yard; girl gathered flowers at a florist; girl received paper flowers from her doll.)

Revisiting the Text

pages 16–17

Concepts of Print

 Capitalize First Word in Sentence; End Punctuation

- Tell children that the words on page 16 show a complete sentence. Ask: *How does each sentence begin? How does each sentence end? What kind of sentence is this? How can you tell?* (telling sentence; it ends with a period.)

I gathered flowers for my mother,

Yo recogía flores para mi mamá,

14

and my doll gathered flowers for me.

y mi muñeca recogía flores para mí.

15

pages 14–15

pages 18–19

Making Predictions

- *What is the next part of the story about? How do you think washing will be alike and different?*

Every time it was the same, but different.

Cada vez era lo mismo, pero diferente.

16

17

pages 16–17

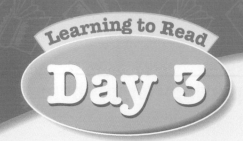

pages 18–19

pages 20–21

pages 22–23

▶ Supporting Comprehension

pages 20–21

Comprehension Focus: Story Structure: Characters/Setting

Student Modeling *Who are the story characters on these pages? How is the setting different in each picture?* (Great-grand-mother washed by the stream and hung the clothes in the trees to dry; the land and animals are more wild. Grandmother washed with water from a well and hung the clothes on a line to dry; the land is now a farm with farm animals.)

Revisiting the Text

page 20

Concepts of Print

Return Sweep; Capitalize First Word in Sentence; End Punctuation

- Read page 20, tracking the print with your hand. Point out that when you reach the end of the line, you return to the beginning of the next line to keep reading. Have volunteers run their hand under the print as you read the words.

- Point to the first word on page 20. *My begins with a capital letter because it is the first word in the sentence. We'll keep reading until we come to the end of the sentence.*

DAY 3

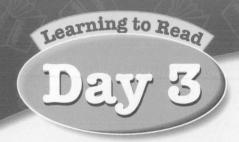

Supporting Comprehension

pages 30–31

Strategy: Evaluate

Student Modeling *Do you think the girl likes pretending she is a mother to her doll? Why do you think that?*

Teacher's Note

The artists for *Tortillas and Lullabies* are Costa Rican. On a rereading, you might highlight picture details—mountains, rain forest, volcanoes, ocean (in volcano picture), lush flora and fauna—that show what Costa Rica is like.

pages 24–25

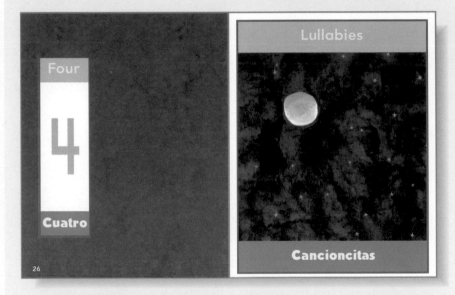

pages 26–27

pages 28–29

My mother sang a lullaby to me,

Mi mamá me cantaba una cancioncita a mí,

30

and I sang a lullaby to my doll —

y yo le cantaba una cancioncita a mi muñeca—

31

pages 30–31

and every time it was the same.

y cada vez fue lo mismo.

32

page 32

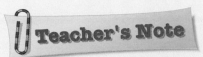
Teacher's Note

If you read Spanish, invite children to listen as you share the book in Spanish. Or, invite a parent or family member who can read Spanish to read the book to the class.

DAY 3

MEETING INDIVIDUAL NEEDS

Challenge

Place the Big Book in an accessible spot so children can look closely at the pictures. Encourage children to find as many similarities and differences as they can in the pictures.

Sharing the Big Book   T33

Learning to Read
Day 3

Practice Book p. 79

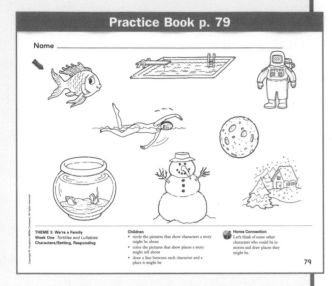

Name _____

THEME 3: We're a Family
Week One *Tortillas and Lullabies*
Characters/Setting, Responding

Children
• circle the pictures that show characters a story might be about
• color the pictures that show places a story might tell about
• draw a line between each character and a place it might be

Home Connection
Let's think of some other characters who could be in stories and draw places they might be.

79

▶ Responding to the Story

Retelling Use these prompts to help children summarize the story:

■ *What family did the author write about?*

■ *What did each picture in the book show?* (a mother-daughter relationship)

■ *Which part of the story did you like best?*

Literature Circle Have small groups discuss some activities that they do today, like washing the dishes. Then ask: *Do you think that when your parents and grandparents were little they washed the dishes the same way that you wash the dishes?*

Practice Book page 79 Children will complete the page at small group time.

Diagnostic Check

If...	You can...
children need more practice in identifying characters and settings,	help them name characters and settings in known stories from the class library.

English Language Learners

Allow less proficient speakers to draw a scene from the story. Help them talk about it. More proficient children can draw themselves in a similar story or show how the story would change if it were about the men in the family.

T34   THEME 3: **We're a Family**

At Group Time
Book Center

Materials • picture books about families

Ask pairs of children to revisit the books about families in the Book Center. As partners browse through the books, have them look at what the characters are doing in each of the books. Have children point out the activities that they do with their own families. Encourage children to talk about these activities with each other.

At Group Time
Art Center

Materials • drawing paper • crayons and markers

Before sending children to the Art Center, make sure they have had a chance to review the books about families in the Book Center. Then have children draw pictures to show an activity that they do, or would like to do, with a family member.

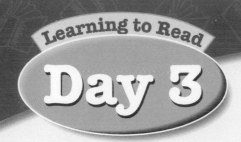

OBJECTIVES

Children

- identify words that begin with /t/
- identify pictures whose names start with the letter *t*

MATERIALS

- **Alphafriend Card** *Tiggy Tiger*
- **Alphafriend Audiotape** Theme 3
- **Letter Cards** *s, t*
- **Picture Cards** for *s, t*

Extra Support

Read "Toaster Time," *Higglety Pigglety: A Book of Rhymes,* page 15. Have children tap their fingers on the table each time they hear a word that begins with /t/. Then call on volunteers to point to words that begin with *t* in the rhyme.

Phonics

✓ Initial Consonant t

▶ Develop Phonemic Awareness

Beginning Sound Read the lyrics to Tiggy Tiger's song aloud, and have children echo it line-for-line. Have them listen for the /t/ words.

Tell children that you will read the poem again. *This time, if you hear a word that begins with /t/, stand up. If you hear another /t/ word, sit down. We'll do this each time, we hear a /t/ word.* As needed, model standing and sitting alternately for /t/ words as you read the first line.

Then say the entire poem, having just children stand and sit for /t/ words.

Tiggy Tiger's Song
(Tune: "Twinkle, Twinkle Little Star")

Tiggy Tiger can tickle his toes.
Tiggy Tiger can tap his nose.
Tiggy Tiger can turn around.
Tiggy Tiger can touch the ground.
Tiggy Tiger can tie his shoes.
Tiggy Tiger can count by twos.

▶ Connect Sounds to Letters

Beginning Letter *t* Display the Tiggy Tiger card and have children name the letter on the picture. *What letter stands for the sound /t/, as in* tiger? *(t) Who can help you remember the sound /t/?* (Tiggy Tiger)

Write *tiger* on the board, underlining the *t*. *What is the first letter in the word* tiger? (t) Tiger *starts /t/, so* t *is the first letter I write for* tiger.

Compare and Review Display the Letter Cards for *t* and *s* on the chalkboard ledge. Review the sound for *s* with children. Then distribute Picture Cards for *s* and *t*, one to a child, to a group of children. In turn, children name their picture, say the beginning sound, and stand by the correct letter on the board ledge. Children without Picture Cards verify the decisions.

Repeat the activity with different groups of children until each child has a chance to name a picture, say the beginning sound, and stand below the correct symbol on the board.

Phonics
in Action

Applying Skills

▶ Introducing the Story

Let's look at the title page. It says "The Birthday Party." We'll look at the pictures to see if we can figure out whose birthday it is. Do you think you would like to be at this party? Why or why not? Together identify pictures whose names start with /t/.

As you do a picture walk, guide children in a discussion of the pictures.

▶ Coached Reading

Have children look carefully at each page before discussing it with you. Prompts:

page 1   How do you know that this is a birthday party? (There are streamers, party hats, and a birthday cake.)

page 2   What is happening in this picture? (The birthday girl is helping her mom set the table and get ready for the party.)

page 3   More guests are here. Who do you think they are? (It is grandma and grandpa!)

page 5   The birthday girl has many presents. Do you think she likes them all? Why or why not? (She is smiling at her family; she likes all of her presents!)

pages 6–7   What is happening in this picture? Why is everyone waving? (The party is over. It is time for grandma and grandpa to go home.)

Now let's go back and look at each page to find things that begin with Tiggy Tiger's sound, /t/.

Purposes
- read a wordless story
- find pictures beginning with /t/

The Birthday Party
by Susan Gorman-Howe
illustrated by Grace Lin

DAY 3

Home Connection

Children can color the pictures in the take-home version of "The Birthday Party." After rereading on Day 4, they can take it home to read to family members.

Responding   (T37)

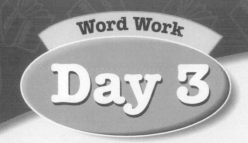

Word Work

Day 3

OBJECTIVES

Children

• explore family words

Exploring Words

....

▶ **Family Words**

Point to the People in a Family chart from yesterday's Vocabulary Expansion activity. Ask: *Can you think of any other family members to add to the chart? Do you call people special names, like* grandpa *or* nana? *Let's add those to the chart, too.*

People in a Family

great-grandmother, bisabuela	great-grandfather, bisabuelo
grandmother, abuela, granny, nana	grandfather, abuelo, grampy, poppop
mother, mamá, mom, mommy	father, papá , dad, daddy, babá
daughter	son
sister	brother
aunt, auntie, tía, théa	uncle, tío, théo

Writing Opportunity Have children create a Family Word Bank in their journals. Children can copy the words that name family members from the People in a Family Chart.

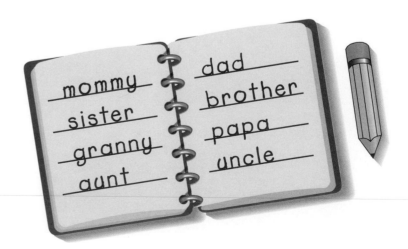

Shared Writing

▶ Recording Observations

Display *Jonathan and His Mommy*. Remind children that Jonathan and his mommy like walking and talking together. Take a picture walk of *Jonathan and His Mommy* and have children retell the story in their own words.

■ Have children make-believe that they are taking a walk with Jonathan and his mommy. Ask: **What kinds of things might you see on your walk?** Record children's answers on chart paper.

We Saw

a rainbow	tall buildings
a spider web	children playing ball
a fountain	construction workers
kids playing music	my street
a brown cat	a coffee shop

Post the chart on the board where children can see it. Then have small groups work together to create murals. Have children draw what they saw on their "walk" with Jonathan and his mommy. Tell children that they can include some of the things on the chart. Children may also think of other things that they might like to include. When groups complete their murals, invite children to share their pictures with the class.

OBJECTIVES

Children
• record observations

MATERIALS

• **Read Aloud Book:** *Jonathan and His Mommy*

DAY 3

Day 4

Day at a Glance

Learning to Read

Big Book:

Families

 Phonics:
Review Initial
Consonant *t*,
page T44

Word Work

Exploring Words, *page T46*

Writing & Language

Interactive Writing, *page T47*

 Half-Day Kindergarten

 Indicates lessons for tested
skills. Choose additional
activities as time allows.

Opening

Calendar

Sunday	Monday	Tuesday	Wednesday	Thursday	Friday	Saturday
			1	2	3	4
5	6	7	8	9	10	11
12	13	14	15	16	17	18
19	20	21	22	23	24	25
26	27	28	29	30	31	

After reciting the days of
the week, ask children if
they have a special day
of the week for family
night or a special meal.
You might volunteer, for
example, that Friday night
is pizza night at your
house.

Daily Message

Interactive Writing Use some
words that begin with *t* in today's
message. Call on volunteers to
circle the *t*'s.

Today we will
eat tacos.

Read the Word Wall together, then play a rhyming game: *I'm going to find
a word on the wall that rhymes with* tree. Tree *rhymes with... see. Raise your
hand when you find a word that rhymes with* pie. *(I, my)*

Daily Phonemic Awareness
Beginning Sounds

- *Listen as I say two words:* tooth, toe. *Say the words with me:* tooth, toe. *Do you hear the same sound at the beginning of each word? Yes,* tooth *and* toe *begin with the same sound.* Help children isolate the beginning sound, /t/.

- Have children play What's the Sound? Explain that you will say two words that begin with the same sound. They should raise their hands when they know the sound.

- Say the following pairs of words. For each pair, have children isolate and identify the beginning sound.

rabbit/riddle
man/mom
talk/tell
son/sister
toast/teeth
rooster/ride

Getting Ready to Learn

To help plan their day, tell children that they will

- read the Social Studies Link: *Families.*

- sort words that begin with *t* in the Phonics Center.

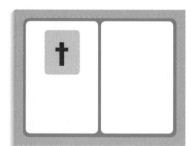

- reread a book called "The Birthday Party."

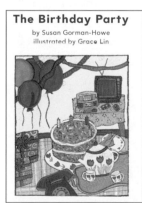

The Birthday Party
by Susan Gorman-Howe
illustrated by Grace Lin

OBJECTIVES ◎

Children

- identify characters and setting in a story

- recognize use of capital letter at the beginning of a sentence

- recognize use of end punctuation: period, question mark

- observe use of directionality: end sweep

Big Book

pages 35–41

Oral Language

celebrate People celebrate special events. Many people celebrate birthdays and holidays. What other events could people celebrate?

Sharing the Big Book
Social Studies Link

▶ **Building Background**

Ask children to tell about ways their family plays together and works together. Read aloud the title and invite children to comment on the cover photograph.

Reading for Understanding Pause for discussion as you share the selection.

> **page 35**
>
> ## Strategy: Evaluate
>
> **Student Modeling** Remind children that good readers think about how they feel when they read a story. Ask: *Does this picture show a real or make-believe family? How does this family picture make you feel?*

page 38
Noting Details

- *What are the mother and daughter doing on page 36?*

page 39
Compare and Contrast

- *Is your family big or small? Which family is most like yours?*

page 40
Noting Details

- *What is each family on this page celebrating? How can you tell?*

Families live together.

36

Families play together.

37

pages 36–37

Families work together.

38

Families can be big or small.

39

pages 38–39

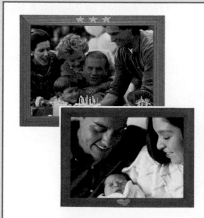

Families celebrate
the old and the new.

40

What does your family do?

41

pages 40–41

Revisiting the Text

pages 38–41

Concepts of Print

✓ **Capitalize First Word in Sentence; End Punctuation; Return Sweep**

■ Frame and read Families work together. **Why does *Families* begin with a capital letter?** (It is the first word of the sentence.) **What mark ends the sentence?**

■ Read aloud the sentence on page 40, running your hand under the words. Then have a volunteer track the print as you reread the sentence. Point out that when the volunteer came to the end of a line, he or she returned to the beginning of the next line to keep reading.

■ Point to the sentence on page 41. **How does this sentence begin? How does it end?** (with a capital letter; with a question mark)

▶ Responding

Personal Response Allow children to respond to the question at the end of the selection. Then ask them to tell about their favorite part of the book.

DAY 4

MEETING INDIVIDUAL NEEDS

Extra Support

Allow children time to examine and talk about each picture. Help them determine if the picture shows families living together, playing together, or working together.

Phonics

✅ Review Initial Consonant t

▶ Develop Phonemic Awareness

Beginning Sound Display the scene in Tiggy Tiger's Alphafolder. *One thing I see is a telephone. Say* telephone *with me. Does* telephone *begin with the same sound as* **Tiggy Tiger,** */t/?* Call on volunteers to point to and name other items in the picture that begin with /t/.

▶ Connect Sounds to Letters

Review Consonant *t* Using self-stick notes, cover the words on page 21 of *From Apples to Zebras: A Book of ABC's.* Then display the page. Ask children what letter they expect to see first in each word and why. Uncover the words so that children can check their predictions.

Provide each child with a self-stick note. Ask children to write the letter *t* on their notes. Then have children take turns placing their notes on objects in the classroom that begin with /t/. Make a word list of the objects children suggest, and have volunteers underline each *t*.

T t

tiger

telephone | toaster

21

From Apples to Zebras: A Book of ABC's, **page 21**

<u>t</u>oy	<u>t</u>ools
<u>t</u>able	<u>t</u>ruck
<u>t</u>eacher	<u>t</u>ractor
<u>t</u>elephone	<u>t</u>rain
<u>t</u>owels	

Home Connection

Challenge children to look at home for items or for names that begin with the consonant *t*. Children can draw pictures to show what they have found.

▶ Apply

Compare and Review: *m, t* In a pocket chart, display the cards for Tiggy Tiger and Mimi Mouse along with the Letter Cards *t* and *m*. Review the sound for *m,* /m/. Place the Picture Cards in the pocket chart in random order. Ask children to name a picture, say the beginning sound, and place the card below the right letter.

Pictures: *toast, map, tent, mix, toys, man*

Tell children they will sort more pictures in the Phonics Center today.

Practice Book page 80 Children will complete this page at small group time.

Phonics Library In groups today, children will also identify pictures that begin with /t/ as they reread the **Phonics Library** story "The Birthday Party." See suggestions, page T37.

Phonics Center

Use the Phonics Center materials for **Theme 3, Week 1, Day 4**.

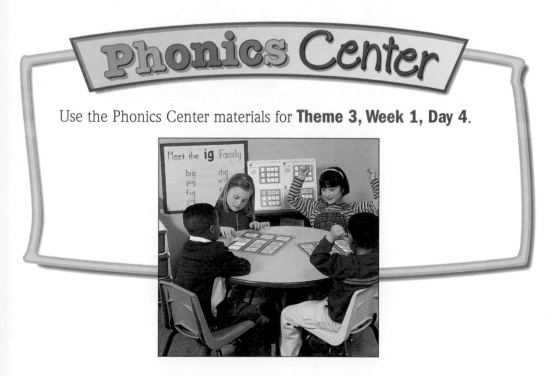

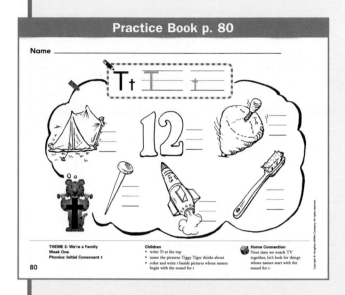
DAY 4

Diagnostic Check

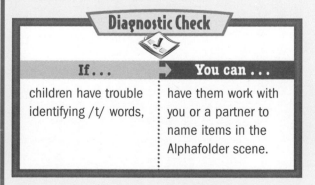

If...	You can ...
children have trouble identifying /t/ words,	have them work with you or a partner to name items in the Alphafolder scene.

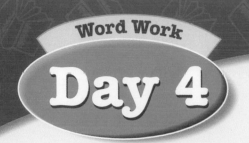

Word Work

Day 4

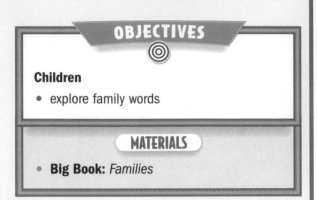

OBJECTIVES

Children
- explore family words

MATERIALS

- **Big Book:** *Families*

Exploring Words

▶ **Family Words**

Display the chart children used during yesterday's Word Work activity. Read the chart with children.

■ Recall with children that the selection *Families* showed different families.

■ Page through the selection, having children name the family members. As they make suggestions, help children find the words on the chart. Add any new words.

■ Then, on a separate piece of chart paper, write the sentences:

> Families live together.
> Families play together.
> Families work together.

Writing Opportunity Place the above chart in the Writing Center. Have children draw a picture of something their family does together. Some children will be able to copy a word or sentence from the chart and label their picture independently. Others may prefer to dictate their sentences.

Interactive Writing

▶ Writing a Journal Entry

Review some of things that Jonathan and his mother saw on their walk. Page through the book to help children remember some of the specifics.

Tell children that today they will help you write a journal entry for Jonathan. Explain that people often keep journals to remember what they have done and seen.

- Start the journal entry with *Today, I went walking with _____. I saw _____.* Ask children to complete the sentences. Then read the sentences aloud.

- Continue the journal entry, calling on children to contribute items. Have children share in the writing. They can write capital *I* and add end punctuation. They can also help you spell words that begin with known consonants.

Today, I went walking
with my mommy.
I saw _____.

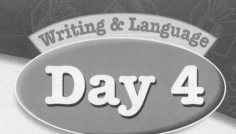

OBJECTIVES

Children
- write a journal entry

MATERIALS

- **Read Aloud:** *Jonathan and His Mommy*

DAY 4

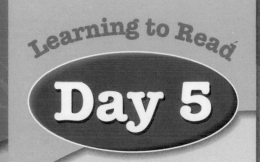

Learning to Read

Day 5

Day at a Glance

Learning to Read

Revisiting the Literature:

Jonathan and His Mommy, Tortillas and Lullabies, Families, "The Birthday Party"

☑ **Phonics Review:** Initial Consonants *m, s, t,* page T52

Word Work

Exploring Words, page T54

Writing & Language

Independent Writing, page T55

 Half-Day Kindergarten

☑ Indicates lessons for tested skills. Choose additional activities as time allows.

Opening

Calendar

Sunday	Monday	Tuesday	Wednesday	Thursday	Friday	Saturday
			1	2	3	4
5	6	7	8	9	10	11
12	13	14	15	16	17	18
19	20	21	22	23	24	25
26	27	28	29	30	31	

After conducting the calendar routine, ask children to share their weekend plans with the class. *What are you planning to do this weekend with your family?*

Daily Message

Interactive Writing As you write the daily message, call on children to help you. *What kind of letter should I use to begin my sentence?... Is this a telling sentence or an asking sentence? How should I end the sentence, with a period or a question mark?*

> Let's look at the books we read this week. What is your favorite book?

Display Word Cards for the words on the Word Wall. Have children match the cards to the words on the Word Wall. After a match is made, have other children chant the spelling of the word: **m-y** *spells* **my.**

Routines

 Daily Phonemic Awareness
Beginning Sounds

- Play a guessing game with children.

- Choose a word that names a family member, for example, *mother*. Say:
  I am thinking of a family member. The word that names this person begins
  with /m/. Which family member has a name that begins with /m/?

- Allow children to guess all the possibilities (*mommy, mom, mamá,* and
  so on) before revealing the word you had in mind.

- Repeat several times with the names of other family members until
  children have caught on to how to play. Then let children take turns
  thinking of words.

Getting Ready to Learn

To help plan their day, tell children that they will

- reread and talk about all the books they've read this week.

- take home a story they can read, "The Birthday Party."

- write about their favorite foods in their journals.

DAY 5

Revisiting the Literature

▶ **Literature Discussion**

Today children will compare the different books you shared this week: *Jonathan and His Mommy*, *Tortillas and Lullabies*, *Families*, and "The Birthday Party." First, use these suggestions to help children recall the selections:

■ Ask children what Jonathan liked to do in *Jonathan and His Mommy*. Have children recall some of the funny ways Jonathan and his mother walked.

■ Display *Tortillas and Lullabies*. Have children tell how the girl's activities are the same and different from the ways in which her mother, grandmother, and great-grandmother did them.

■ Have children recall *Families*. Call on volunteers to find activities in the selection that they do with their own families.

■ Together, read "The Birthday Party." Ask volunteers to name the /t/ pictures in the illustrations.

■ Ask children to vote for their favorite book of the week. Then read aloud the text of the winner.

✓ Comprehension Focus: Story Structure: Characters/Setting

Comparing Books Remind children that good readers pay attention to important story parts such as characters, who the story is about, and setting, where the story takes place. Display each selection and have children recall the main characters. Then browse through each selection, inviting children to comment on the setting. For example, children might comment that Jonathan and his mother live in a city neighborhood while the girl in *Tortillas and Lullabies* lives in a country setting.

www.eduplace.com
Log on to **Education Place** for more activities relating to We're a Family.

www.bookadventure.org
This Internet reading-incentive program provides thousands of titles for children to read.

Building Fluency

▶ Rereading Familiar Texts

Phonics Library: "The Birthday Party" Remind children that they've learned the sound for *t*, /t/. As children reread the Phonics Library story "The Birthday Party," have them look for pictures that begin with /t/.

Review Feature several familiar Phonics Library titles in the Book Corner. Have children demonstrate their growing skills by choosing one to describe the pictures, alternating pages with a partner.

Oral Reading Frequent rereadings of familiar texts help children develop their vocabulary. Model how to describe the illustration expressively. Then have children try it.

Blackline Master 36 Children complete the page and take it home to share their reading progress.

The Birthday Party
by Susan Gorman-Howe
illustrated by Grace Lin

My Red Boat
by Susan Gorman-Howe
illustrated by Lauren Scheuer

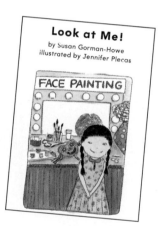

Look at Me!
by Susan Gorman-Howe
illustrated by Jennifer Plecas

My Reading Log

I can read

My new words

_my_

DAY 5

Home Connection

Remind children to share the **take-home** version of "The Birthday Party" with their families.

Phonics Review

☑ Initial Consonants: m, s, t

Children

- review initial consonants *m, s, t*
- make sentences with high-frequency words

MATERIALS

- **Word Cards** *I, see, my*
- **Punctuation Card:** period
- **Picture Cards** for *m, s, t;* and others for sentence building

▶ Review

Tell children that they will take turns naming pictures and telling what letter stands for the beginning sound.

- ■ Randomly place four Picture Cards along the chalkboard ledge. Write *m, s,* and *t* on the board. Then call on four children to come up and stand in front of each picture. In turn, have each child name the picture, isolate the initial sound, and point to *m, s,* or *t* on the chalkboard.

- ■ Have the rest of the class verify that the correct letter has been chosen. Then write the picture name on the board and underline the initial consonant.

- ■ Continue until everyone has a chance to name a picture and point to the consonant that stands for its beginning sound.

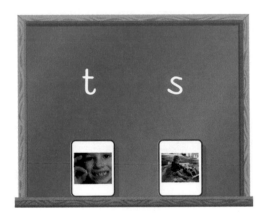

High-Frequency Word Review

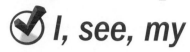 *I, see, my*

▶ Review

Give each small group the Word Cards, Picture Cards, and Punctuation Card needed to make a sentence. Each child holds one card. Children stand and arrange themselves to make a sentence for others to read.

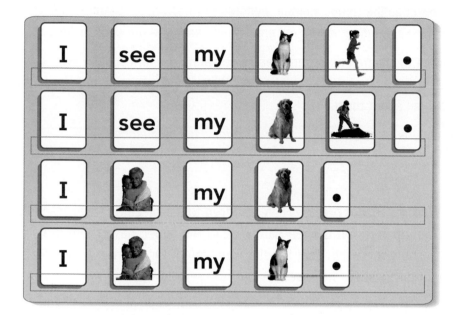

▶ Apply

Practice Book page 81 Children can complete this page independently and read it to you during small group time.

Phonics Library Have children take turns reading aloud to the class. Each child might describe one page of "The Birthday Party" or a favorite **Phonics Library** selection from the previous theme. Remind readers to share the pictures! Discussion questions:

■ *Find a picture that starts with the same sound as Tiggy Tiger's name. What is the letter? What is the sound?*

■ *Can you find any pictures that begin with the same sound as Reggie Rooster or Sammy Seal?*

Practice Book p. 81

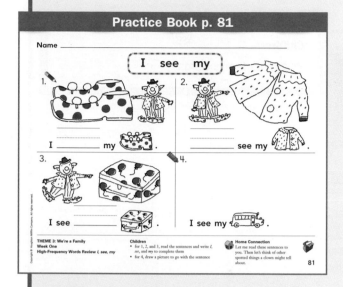

Portfolio Opportunity

Save the Practice Book page to show children's recognition of high-frequency words.

Diagnostic Check

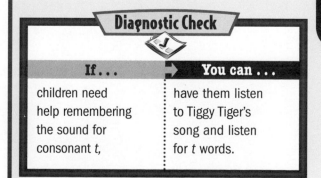

If . . .	You can . . .
children need help remembering the sound for consonant *t*,	have them listen to Tiggy Tiger's song and listen for *t* words.

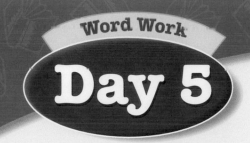

Exploring Words

▶ Family Words

Remind children that they have been talking about families. Display page 40 of *Families*. Call on volunteers to name the family members in the picture and describe what event is being celebrated.

■ Discuss events children have celebrated. Prompt children to name events such as birthdays, weddings, anniversaries, holidays, and graduations. Have children acknowledge the family member honored or involved, for example: *We celebrated Aunt Tina's wedding. It was my great-grandmother's ninetieth birthday.*

■ Mention to children that many people celebrate or mark special events by sending cards. Have those children who have received cards, such as birthday cards, tell about them.

■ Tell children that they will make a card for a family member.

Writing Opportunity Have children fold a piece of paper in half and then open it. On the left hand side of the paper, have them draw a picture to show the event that is being celebrated. On the right-hand side, have children dictate a message.

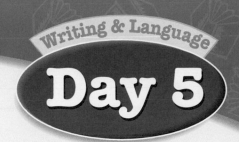
Independent Writing

Journals Review this week's shared and interactive writing posted in the classroom. Point out the different family words and naming words children used. Tell children that today they will write about a favorite family activity.

- Pass out the journals.

- *Let's discuss some of the things we read about this week. What were some things Jonathan did with his mommy? What did the girl in* Tortillas and Lullabies *do with her mother? What family activities did we read about in* Families?

- Recall with children the journal entry they wrote for *Jonathan and His Mommy.* Then suggest that children draw and write about favorite family activities. Each child can draw a picture and dictate a label describing it.

- If children write a sentence using the words posted around the room, remind them to begin their sentences with capital letters and to end each sentence with a period or a question mark.

- If time permits, have children share what they've written with a partner.

DAY 5

Literature for Week 2
Different texts for different purposes

Goldilocks and the Three Bears

Teacher Read Aloud

Purposes

- oral language
- listening strategy
- comprehension skill

Big Books:

Higglety Pigglety: A Book of Rhymes

Purposes

- oral language development
- phonemic awareness

From Apples to Zebras: A Book of ABC's

Purposes

- alphabet recognition
- letters and sounds

HOUGHTON MIFFLIN
Reading **SHOES FROM GRANDPA**
by MEM FOX • Illustrated by PATRICIA MULLINS

Includes: Social Studies Link

Big Book: **Main Selection**

Purposes

- concepts of print
- reading strategy
- story language
- comprehension skills

 Award

★ Library of Congress Children's Books of the Year

Also available in Little Big Book and audiotape

Leveled Books

Social Studies Link

Which Would You Choose?

33

Also in the Big Book:
- Social Studies Link

Purposes

- reading strategies
- comprehension skills
- concepts of print

Phonics Library

HOUGHTON MIFFLIN
Reading

Phonics Library

We're a Family

Also available in Take-Home version

Purpose

- applying phonics skills and high-frequency words

On My Way Paperback

On My Way
Practice Readers

Nicky Takes a Bath
by **Sam Fonte**
page T157

Little Readers for Guided Reading
Collection K

Houghton Mifflin Classroom Bookshelf
Level K

Technology

www.eduplace.com

Log on to *Education Place* for more activities relating to *We're a Family*.

www.bookadventure.org

This free Internet reading incentive program provides thousands of titles for students to read.

Suggested Daily Routines

Instructional Goals

Learning to Read

☑ *Phonemic Awareness:* Beginning Sounds

Strategy Focus: Predict/Infer

☑ *Comprehension Skill:* Inferences: Drawing Conclusions

☑ *Phonics Skills*

Phonemic Awareness: Beginning Sound /b/

Initial Consonant *B, b*

Compare and Review: Initial Consonant: *t*

☑ *High-Frequency Word: like*

☑ *Concepts of Print:* Capitalize First Word in Sentences; End Punctuation; Return Sweep

Word Work

High-Frequency Word Practice: Family Words, Building Sentences

Writing & Language

Vocabulary Skills: Using Exact Naming Words, Types of Clothing

Writing Skills: Writing a Grocery List, Choosing a Good Title

☑ = tested skills

📖 Leveled Books

Have children read in appropriate levels daily.

Phonics Library
On My Way Practice Readers
Little Big Books
Houghton Mifflin Classroom Bookshelf

Day 1

Opening Routines, *T62–T63*

Word Wall
• **Phonemic Awareness:** Beginning Sounds

Teacher Read Aloud
Goldilocks and the Three Bears, T64–T67
• **Strategy:** Predict/Infer
• **Comprehension:** Inferences: Drawing Conclusions

Phonics
Instruction
• Phonemic Awareness, Beginning Sound /b/, *T68–T69; Practice Book,* 85–86

High-Frequency Word Practice
• Words: *I, see, my, T70*

Oral Language
• Using Exact Naming Words, *T71*
• Viewing and Speaking, *T71*

Managing Small Groups
Teacher-Led Group
• Reread familiar **Phonics Library** selections

Independent Groups
• Finish *Practice Book,* 83–86
• *Phonics Center:* Theme 3, Week 2, Day 1
• Dramatic Play, Writing, other Centers

Day 2

Opening Routines, *T72–T73*

Word Wall
• **Phonemic Awareness:** Beginning Sounds

Sharing the Big Book
Shoes from Grandpa, T74–T75
• **Strategy:** Predict/Infer
• **Comprehension:** Inferences: Drawing Conclusions

Phonics
Instruction, Practice
• Initial Consonant *b, T76–T77*
• *Practice Book,* 87

High-Frequency Word
• New Word: *like, T78–T79*
• *Practice Book,* 88

High-Frequency Word Practice
• Building Sentences, *T80*

Vocabulary Expansion
• Types of Clothing, *T81*
• Viewing and Speaking, *T81*

Managing Small Groups
Teacher-Led Group
• Begin *Practice Book, 87–88* and handwriting Blackline Masters 158 or 184.

Independent Groups
• Finish *Practice Book, 87–88* and handwriting Blackline Masters 158 or 184.
• *Phonics Center:* Theme 3, Week 2, Day 2
• Math, Art, other Centers

Technology

Lesson Planner CD-ROM: Customize your planning for *We're Family* with the Lesson Planner.

Day 3

Opening Routines, *T82–T83*

Word Wall
- **Phonemic Awareness:** Beginning Sounds

Sharing the Big Book
Shoes from Grandpa, T84–T89
- **Strategy:** Predict/Infer
- **Comprehension:** Inferences: Drawing Conclusions, *T86; Practice Book,* 89
- **Concepts of Print:** Capitalize First Word in Sentence, *T85;* Return Sweep; End Punctuation, *T87*

Phonics
Practice, Application
- Initial Consonant *b, T92–T93*

Instruction
- Beginning Letter *b, T92–T93*
- **Phonics Library:** "Baby Bear's Family," *T93*

Exploring Words
- Family Words, *T94*

✏️ **Shared Writing**
- Writing a Grocery List, *T95*
- Listening and Speaking, *T95*

Managing Small Groups
Teacher-Led Group
- Read **Phonics Library** selection "Baby Bear's Family"
- Begin *Practice Book,* 89

Independent Groups
- Finish *Practice Book,* 61
- Math, Art, other Centers

Day 4

Opening Routines, *T96–T97*

Word Wall
- **Phonemic Awareness:** Beginning Sounds

Sharing the Big Book
Social Studies Link: "Which Would You Choose?," *T98–T99*
- **Strategy:** Infer/Predict
- **Comprehension:** Inferences: Drawing Conclusions
- **Concepts of Print:** Capitalize First Word in Sentence; End Punctuation; Return Sweep

Phonics
Practice
- Review Initial Consonant *b, T100–T101; Practice Book,* 90

Exploring Words
- Family Words, *T102*

✏️ **Interactive Writing**
- Choosing a Good Title, *T103*
- Speaking, *T103*

Managing Small Groups
Teacher-Led Group
- Reread **Phonics Library** selection "Baby Bear's Family"
- Begin *Practice Book,* 90

Independent Groups
- Finish *Practice Book,* 90
- *Phonics Center:* Theme 3, Week 2, Day 4
- Dramatic Play, other Centers

Day 5

Opening Routines, *T104–T105*

Word Wall
- **Phonemic Awareness:** Beginning Sounds

Revisiting the Literature
Comprehension: Inferences: Drawing Conclusions, *T106*
Building Fluency
- **Phonics Library:** "Baby Bear's Family," *T107*

Phonics
Review
- Initial Consonants: *b, m, r, t, T108*

High-Frequency Word Review
- Words: *I, like, my, see, T109; Practice Book,* 91

Exploring Words
- Family Words, *T110*

✏️ **Independent Writing**
- Journals, *T111*

Managing Small Groups
Teacher-Led Group
- Reread familiar **Phonics Library** selections
- Begin *Practice Book,* 91, Blackline Master 36.

Independent Groups
- Reread **Phonics Library** selections
- Finish *Practice Book,* 91, Blackline Master 36.
- Centers

Setting up the Centers

Phonics Center

Materials • Phonics Center materials for Theme 3, Week 2

Pairs work together to sort Picture Cards by initial sound. See pages T69, T77, and T101 for this week's Phonics Center activities.

Writing Center

Materials • Types of Clothing chart • drawing paper • markers

Children refer to the clothing chart and then draw and label pictures of their clothing. See page T71 for this week's Writing Center activity.

jeans   shirt

Dramatic Play Center

Materials • 3 bowls • 3 chairs • 3 mats for beds • paper and pencils • grocery circulars

Children will enjoy working in small groups to dramatize the story *Goldilocks and the Three Bears.* Later in the week they write grocery lists for different family events. See page T65 and T103 for this week's Dramatic Play Center activities.

Teacher's Note

Ask families to send in grocery circulars for children to use when writing their grocery lists.

Party List
birthday cake
ice cream
hats
plates

Math Center

Materials • chart paper • paper squares • markers • glue • magazines • scissors

Children make a graph showing the types of shoes they are wearing. Later in the week they sort pictures of clothing into different categories. See pages T75 and T91 for this week's Math Center activities.

See Our Shoes

Kiesha		
Andrew		
Justin		Paul
Carly	Ashley	Jamie
sneaker	slip-on shoe	boot

Art Center

Materials • markers and crayons • drawing paper • Blackline Master 91

Children draw pictures of themselves engaging in a winter activity and in a summer activity. Later in the week, they also draw and label a picture of a favorite present. See T81 and T91 for this week's Art Center activities.

Summer

Winter

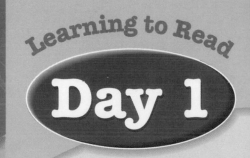

Learning to Read

Day 1

Day at a Glance

Learning to Read

Read Aloud:

Goldilocks and the Three Bears

 Learning About / b /, *page T68*

Word Work

High-Frequency Word Practice, *page T70*

Writing & Language

Oral Language, *page T71*

 Half-Day Kindergarten

 Indicates lessons for tested skills. Choose additional activities as time allows.

Opening

Calendar

Sunday	Monday	Tuesday	Wednesday	Thursday	Friday	Saturday
			1	2	3	4
5	6	7	8	9	10	11
12	13	14	15	16	17	18
19	20	21	22	23	24	25
26	27	28	29	30	31	

Point out the preceding Saturday and Sunday, and invite children to share what they did with their families over the weekend. Compare the number of school days and weekend days. *How many more school days are there than weekend days?*

Daily Message

Interactive Writing Incorporate children's news into the daily message. Have children share the pen by writing their own names.

Jamie and Andres went on a picnic. We will eat a snack outside today!

Have children chant the spelling of each word on the wall today: *capital* I *spells* I, m-y *spells* my, s-e-e *spells* see.

✓ Daily Phonemic Awareness
Beginning Sounds

- Tell children that they will now play Same Sound Sort.
  I will say two words. Listen carefully to find out if the two words begin with the same sound.

- Remind children that if the words begin with the same sound, they should raise their hands. If the words do not begin with the same sound, they should cover their ears.

socks/soup	little/light
moss/pencil	bat/bike
car/puppy	hand/cat
four/find	toad/time

Getting Ready to Learn

To help plan their day, tell children that they will

- listen to a story called *Goldilocks and the Three Bears.*

- meet a new Alphafriend, Benny Bear.

- act out a story in the Dramatic Play Center.

Read Aloud

Purposes • oral language • listening strategy • comprehension skill

Selection Summary
In this classic retelling, Goldilocks enters the home of three bears and proceeds to eat Baby Bear's porridge, break his chair, and fall asleep in his bed before the bears return home to find Goldilocks.

Key Concepts
Relationship of sizes

English Language Learners

Children may not be familiar with the story of *Goldilocks and the Three Bears.* Before reading, share a picture book version of the story with children, using the pictures to build vocabulary and background.

Teacher Read Aloud
Oral Language/Comprehension

▶ **Building Background**

Tell children that the next story they will hear is a fairy tale called *Goldilocks and the Three Bears.* Ask children if they have heard the story before. Discuss *bears*, which are mentioned in the title.

Strategy: Predict/Infer

Teacher Modeling Model the Predict/Infer strategy as you display the selection illustration.

Think Aloud

How can I predict what this story is about? First, I know from the title that this story is about Goldilocks and three bears. When I look at the picture, I see a girl sitting in a chair. This must be Goldilocks because she isn't a bear. As I read, I'll check to see if I'm right.

Comprehension Focus: Inferences: Drawing Conclusions

Teacher Modeling Tell children that good readers use picture clues along with things they know about the story to make decisions about it. Model how to draw conclusions.

Think Aloud

I wonder where Goldilocks is. I don't think Goldilocks is at her own home. I think she is in the bears' home. Do you know how I know this? I see a family picture, and it shows three bears. Goldilocks probably would not have a family picture of bears in her house, so this must be the bears' house.

▶ Listening to the Story

Read the story aloud, using different voices to differentiate the bears and their relative sizes. Pause at the discussion points and allow children to predict what they think will happen next. Note that the Read Aloud art is also available on the back of the Theme Poster.

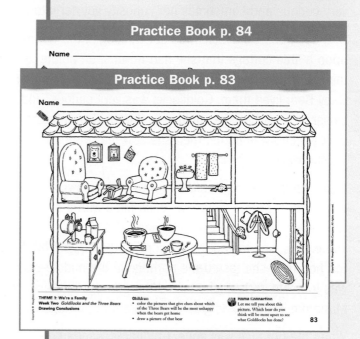

▶ Responding

Summarizing the Story Help children summarize parts of the story.

- *Where were the bears when Goldilocks came to their house?*

- *What did Goldilocks do when she saw the porridge?*

- *What did Goldilocks do next? What happened to Baby Bear's chair?*

- *Where did Goldilocks go next? Where did she fall asleep?*

- *What happened when the three bears came back home?*

- *What do you think Goldilocks' mother said when she heard what happened?*

Practice Book pages 83–84 Children will complete the pages during small group time.

Practice Book p. 84

Name _____

Practice Book p. 83

Name _____

THEME 3: We're a Family
Week Two Goldilocks and the Three Bears
Drawing Conclusions

Children
• color the pictures that give clues about which of the Three Bears will be the most unhappy when the bears get home
• draw a picture of that bear

Home Connection
Let me tell you about this picture. Which bear do you think will be most upset to see what Goldilocks has done?

83

At Group Time

🎭 Dramatic Play Center

Materials • 3 bowls • 3 chairs • 3 mats for beds

Set up the Center with props to act out *Goldilocks and the Three Bears.* Have groups of four act out the story. Other children can be the audience.

📎 Teacher's Note

Mention to children that many fairy tales have "threes" in them. Brainstorm fairy tale titles that show this, for example, *The Three Little Pigs* and *The Three Billy Goats Gruff*. Other fairy tales have "threes" as important parts in a story—three wishes, three fairies, three trials, or three visits. As you share fairy tales with children, ask them to listen for "threes."

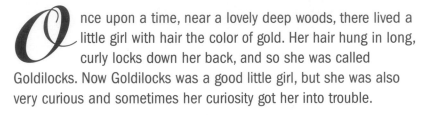

Goldilocks and the Three Bears

A Fairy Tale

Once upon a time, near a lovely deep woods, there lived a little girl with hair the color of gold. Her hair hung in long, curly locks down her back, and so she was called Goldilocks. Now Goldilocks was a good little girl, but she was also very curious and sometimes her curiosity got her into trouble.

One day when Goldilocks was out walking in the woods, she came upon a little cottage that she had never seen before. She didn't know this, but it belonged to the three bears—Mama Bear, Papa Bear, and Baby Bear lived there. Goldilocks was very curious, and so she went closer to see what she could see. She peeked into the kitchen window. No one was home. Then she saw that the door was wide open. So she walked right in!

There, on the kitchen table was a wee, tiny bowl, a middle-sized bowl, and a great, huge bowl—each filled with a hot cereal called "porridge." Seeing the porridge made Goldilocks hungry so she ate some. First, she tasted the porridge in the biggest bowl—but it was too hot. Then she tasted the porridge in the middle-sized bowl—but it was too cold. At last, she tasted the porridge in the smallest bowl—Mmmmm, it was just right, so she ate that porridge all up.

When the porridge was gone, Goldilocks wandered into the living room. There she saw three chairs—each one a different size. **(Say: *What do you think Goldilocks will do?*)** Goldilocks tried to climb into the biggest chair—but it was too high. Next, she tried the middle-sized chair—but it was too wide. So finally, Goldilocks tried the smallest one—Ohhhhh, as you might suspect, that chair was just right. But she sat down just a little too hard, and the chair broke into little pieces!

In the next room, Goldilocks saw three neatly made beds. They looked so comfortable she thought, "Maybe I'll just take a little rest." So first she tried the biggest bed—but it was too hard. She tried the middle-sized bed—but it was too soft. When she finally tried the smallest bed,—Ahhhhh! Goldilocks found that it was just right. And she fell right to sleep. **(Ask: *Was this a good idea? Why or why not?*)**

Now do you know who owned that cottage? It was a family of bears. There was a great, huge Papa Bear, a middle-sized Mama Bear, and a wee, tiny Baby Bear. They were taking a walk in the woods while their porridge cooled. Soon the family of bears came home.

In the kitchen, the bears knew right away that something was wrong. Papa Bear noticed that someone had been tasting his porridge. He frowned and said in his deep, loud voice, "Someone's been eating my porridge!" Mama Bear noticed that someone had been tasting her porridge, too. She wrinkled her forehead and said in her middle-sized voice, "Someone has been eating my porridge!" But Baby Bear cried loudly, "Someone's been eating my porridge, and it's all gone!"

Then they went into the living room. **(Ask: *What will the bears see?*)** Well, it didn't take long for Papa Bear to notice that someone had been sitting in his big chair. He frowned. "Someone has been sitting in my chair!" he said in his deep, loud voice. Mama Bear noticed that someone had been sitting in her chair, too. She wrinkled her forehead again. "Someone has been sitting in my chair," she said. But when Baby Bear saw his little chair, he cried, "Someone's been sitting in my chair, and it's broken!"

Finally, they went into the bedroom. **(Ask: *You know what they saw here. How did you know?*)** And there, Papa Bear noticed right away that someone had been sleeping in his big bed. He frowned. "Someone has been sleeping in my bed!" he said. Mama Bear saw that someone had been sleeping in her bed, too. She wrinkled her forehead. "Someone has been sleeping in my bed, too!" she said. When Baby Bear saw his bed, he exclaimed, "Someone's been sleeping in my bed, and here she is!"

Goldilocks opened her eyes and saw the bears looking at her. She was so scared that she jumped up, ran past the Baby Bear, out the door, and through the woods until she was home. And she never, never, never again went into a house when no one was at home. Goldilocks had learned her lesson.

When Goldilocks told her mother about what happened, you can imagine what her mother said. **(Ask: *What do you think her mother said?*)**

Teacher Read Aloud

OBJECTIVES

Children

- identify pictures whose names begin with /b/

MATERIALS

- **Alphafriend Cards** *Benny Bear, Tiggy Tiger*
- **Alphafriend Audiotape** Theme 3
- **Alphafolder** *Benny Bear*
- **Picture Cards** *ball, berries, bug, tent, tooth, toys*
- **Phonics Center:** Theme 3, Week 2, Day 1

Home Connection

A take-home version of for Benny Bear's Song is on an **Alphafriends Blackline Master.** Children can share the song with their families.

English Language Learners

Display several Picture Cards for *b*. As you say the picture names, exaggerate the /b/ sounds. Have children hold their hands in front of their mouths to feel the air exhaling.

Phonemic Awareness
✓ Beginning Sound

▶ Introducing the Alphafriend: Benny Bear

Recall that Alphafriends help children to remember the sounds the letters of the alphabet make. Tell children that today they will meet a new Alphafriend. Have children listen as you share a riddle to help them guess who their new Alphafriend is.

1 **Alphafriend Riddle** Read these clues:

- *Our Alphafriend's sound is /b/. Say it with me: /b/.*
- *This animal lives in the woods and sleeps in caves.*
- *He likes to eat berries and fish, but his favorite treat is honey!*
- *You might sleep with a stuffed one of these when you go to bed.*

When most hands are up, call on children until they guess *bear.*

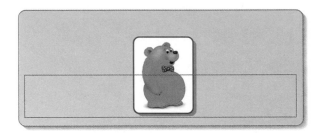

2 **Pocket Chart** Display Benny Bear in a pocket chart. Say his name, emphasizing the /b/ sound slightly, and have children echo.

3 🎞 **Alphafriend Audiotape** Play Benny Bear's song. *Listen for /b/ words in Benny's song.*

4 **Alphafolder** Have children look at the scene and name all the /b/ pictures.

5 **Summarize**

- *What is our Alphafriend's name? What is his sound?*
- *What words in our Alphafriend's song start with /b/?*
- *Each time you look at Benny this week, remember the /b/ sound.*

Benny Bear's Song
(Tune: "Three Blind Mice")

Benny Bear, Benny Bear.
Please beware! Please beware!
I see a bee near the basket
  of beets.
The bee is buzzing by
  buttery treats!
Please don't run. Eat your bun!

▶ Listening for /b/

Compare and Review: /t/ Display Alphafriend *Tiggy Tiger* opposite *Benny Bear.* Review each character's sound.

Hold up the Picture Cards one at a time. Children signal "thumbs up" for pictures that start with Benny Bear's sound, /b/. Volunteers put the cards below Benny's picture. For "thumbs down" words, volunteers put the cards below Tiggy's picture.

Pictures: *tent, ball, tooth, berries, bug, toys, bike*

Practice Book p. 86

Name

Practice Book p. 85

Name

Tell children they will sort more pictures in the Phonics Center today.

▶ Apply

Practice Book pages 85–86 Children will complete the pages at small group time.

At Group Time

Phonics Center

Use the Phonics Center materials for **Theme 3, Week 2, Day 1**.

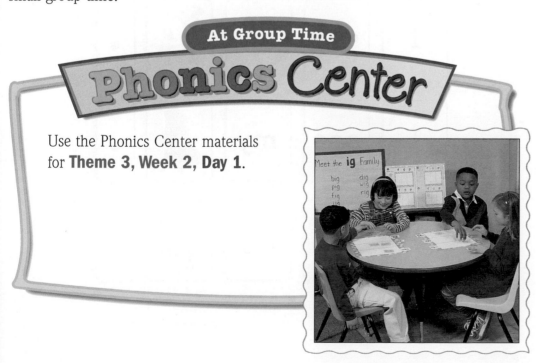

Word Work

Day 1

OBJECTIVES

Children

- read high-frequency words
- create and write sentences with high-frequency words

MATERIALS

- **Word Cards** *I, see, my*
- **Picture Cards** *cat, dog, toys*
- ***Higglety Pigglety: A Book of Rhymes,*** page 12
- **Punctuation Card:** period

High-Frequency Word Practice

▶ **Matching Words**

■ Display Word Cards for the high-frequency words *I*, *see*, and *my* in a pocket chart. Call on children to identify each word and to match it on the Word Wall.

■ *I'll read a poem. You listen to hear if these words are used in it.*

■ Read the poem "I Went Upstairs" on page 12 of *Higglety Pigglety.* *Did you hear any of these words in the poem? Let's see which Word Cards you can match to the words in the poem.* (*I, my*)

I Went Upstairs

I went upstairs to make my bed.
I made a mistake and bumped my head.
I went downstairs to milk my cow.
I made a mistake and milked the sow.
I went to the kitchen to bake a pie.
I made a mistake and baked a fly.

a Jump-Rope Rhyme

12

Higglety Pigglety: A Book of Rhymes, page 12

Writing Opportunity Place the Word Cards *I see my* in a pocket chart as a sentence stem. Have children read the words with you. Then display assorted Picture Cards and ask children to use them to complete the sentence. Children can write and illustrate one of the sentences or use the words to create their own sentences with rebus pictures.

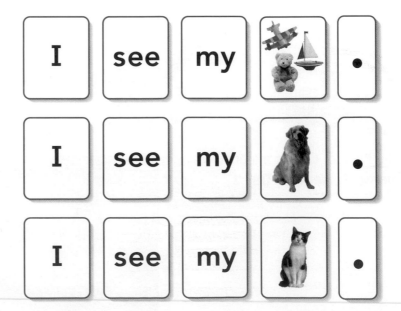

Oral Language

▶ Using Exact Naming Words

Viewing and Speaking Remind children that some words are naming words, or nouns. *Let's think of a naming word. Look around you. I see all of our clothes. Is* clothes *a naming word? Yes,* clothes *is a naming word!*

- Have children look at what they are wearing. *Let's name some types of clothes.* Have children suggest specific articles of clothing. List their ideas on chart paper.

- Read through the list together and tell children that all of the words are more exact naming words.

Types of Clothing

pants	dress
jeans	skirt
shorts	shirt

OBJECTIVES

Children
- use exact nouns to name clothing
- draw and label clothing pictures

Portfolio Opportunity
Save children's work as examples of their drawing and labeling abilities.

At Group Time

Writing Center

Materials • drawing paper • crayons or markers

Put the Types of Clothing chart in the Writing Center. Children can read it on their own or with a partner. During group time, children can draw and label pictures of what they are wearing. Encourage children to refer to the chart to write their words. Some children may also wish to label the colors of their clothing. Make sure the Color Chart from Theme 2 is posted in the Writing Center.

jeans   shirt

English Language Learners

Give children sets of pictures with different articles of clothing and pictures that show different kinds of weather. As they share their groupings, review or introduce vocabulary.

Day at a Glance

Learning to Read

Big Book:

Shoes From Grandpa

☑ Phonics:
Initial
Consonant *b*,
page T76

☑ High-Frequency Word: *like*,
page T78

Word Work

High-Frequency Word Practice,
page T80

Writing & Language

Vocabulary Expansion, *page T81*

 Half-Day Kindergarten

☑ Indicates lessons for tested
skills. Choose additional
activities as time allows.

Opening

Calendar

Sunday	Monday	Tuesday	Wednesday	Thursday	Friday	Saturday
			1	2	3	4
5	6	7	8	9	10	11
12	13	14	15	16	17	18
19	20	21	22	23	24	25
26	27	28	29	30	31	

As you conduct the calendar
routine and examine the
day's weather, incorporate
clothing into the discussion.
*What kind of clothes do we
wear in cool, breezy weather—
a T-shirt or a jacket? shorts or
pants?*

Daily Message

Interactive Writing Share the pen
with children. Have them write
initial consonants for known sounds
and help you spell high-frequency
words.

Today, I wore a
sweater to school.
Seven children did,
too.

Word Wall

Distribute Word Cards for the known high-frequency words. Have children
match the cards to the words on the Word Wall. After a match is made,
have other children chant the spelling of the word. Repeat a few times, distributing the cards to different volunteers.

Daily Phonemic Awareness
Beginning Sounds

- Read "Baa, Baa, Black Sheep" on page 16 of *Higglety Pigglety*.

- Tell children that they will play a game with beginning sounds. *I will say a word from the poem. You listen for the beginning sound and tell me the sound your hear. Now listen:* boy.

- When most hands are up, have children voice the sound. *Yes, /b/ is the sound at the beginning of* boy.

- Continue in a similar manner with other words from the poem: *wool, bags, full, sir, master, dame, lane.*

Baa, Baa, Black Sheep

Baa, baa, black sheep,
Have you any wool?
Yes, sir, yes, sir,
Three bags full,
One for the master,
One for the dame,
One for the little boy
Who lives in the lane.

a Mother Goose Rhyme

Higglety Pigglety: A Book of Rhymes, page 16

Getting Ready to Learn

To help plan their day, tell children that they will

- listen to a Big Book: *Shoes From Grandpa.*

- learn the new letters, *B* and *b*, and see words that begin with b.

- make a graph about shoes in the Math Center.

DAY 2

Big Book

Purposes • concepts of print • story language • reading strategy • comprehension skill

Selection Summary

In this cumulative text story, Grandpa's offer to buy Jessie new shoes this winter has the whole family offering to buy different articles of clothing until they've fashioned a fanciful outfit for Jessie. Jessie, however, just wants a pair of jeans.

Key Concepts

Kinds of clothing

 English Language Learners

The complex sentences and inferential thinking may make this a challenging story for some children. Review or introduce the clothing vocabulary that appears in the story. Also review family vocabulary.

Sharing the Big Book
Oral Language/Comprehension

▶ **Building Background**

Ask if children have ever received clothing as a gift. *Do you like getting clothes as a gift? Why or why not? Would you rather pick out your own clothes? Why?* Then introduce *Shoes From Grandpa* by reading the title and the names of the author and illustrator.

Strategy: Predict/Infer

Teacher Modeling Model how to predict by previewing the title and pictures.

 Think Aloud

Before reading, I like to predict what a story is about.

- *The title tells me that someone gets shoes from Grandpa. I think the man on the cover is Grandpa. The girl must be the one who gets the shoes.*

- *When I look at the pictures in the story, I see this girl and lots of other people. I wonder if they are part of the girl's family, too. When I read, I'll see if I'm right.*

Comprehension Focus:
Inferences: Drawing Conclusions

Teacher Modeling Recall that good readers use what they already know, along with the picture clues, to make decisions about a story. Demonstrate this with pages 2–5 of the story.

Think Aloud

When I look at these pages, I can use picture clues to decide what season it is. The man is wearing shorts and cooking outside, and the next page shows people wearing T-shirts, bathing suits, and other summer clothing. I think the story must happen in the summer. As I read, I will look for more clues that help me make decisions about the story.

▶ Sharing the Story

Read the selection aloud, emphasizing the rhyming words in each line. Pause for children to comment on the pictures.

▶ Responding

Personal Response Encourage children to use the language of the story as they react to it.

- *Everyone in Jessie's family wanted to buy something to go with the shoes from Grandpa. Which gift did you like best? Why?*

- *Which gift did you think was the funniest?*

- *What gift did Jessie really want? Which gift would you want?*

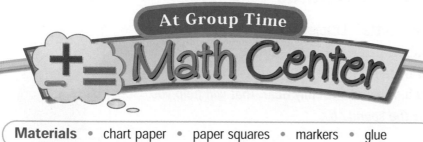

At Group Time

Math Center

Materials • chart paper • paper squares • markers • glue

Have children make a graph that shows the type of shoes they wore to school. Ask children to determine the labels for the shoes on the graph, and label the graph accordingly. During group time, each child can write his or her name on a square of paper and glue it in the correct column. Discuss the graph during a whole group session.

See Our Shoes

Kiesha		
Andrew		
Justin		Paul
Carly	Ashley	Jamie
sneaker	slip-on shoe	boot

Extra Support

Some children may have trouble understanding the time shift in the story. Explain that Jessie's family says they *will* buy these things to go with the shoes from Grandpa, which he *will* buy in the winter. Jessie is imagining these gifts.

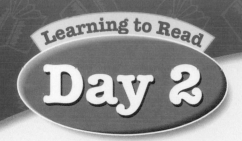
Extra Support

To help children remember the sound for *b*, point out that the letter's name gives a clue to its sound: *b*, / b /.

Phonics

✓ Initial Consonant b

▶ Develop Phonemic Awareness

Beginning Sound Read the lyrics to Benny Bear's song and have children echo it line-for-line. Have them listen for / b / words and "bob" their heads each time they hear one.

> **Benny Bear's Song**
> (Tune: "Three Blind Mice")
> Benny Bear, Benny Bear.
> Please beware! Please beware!
> I see a bee near the basket
>   of beets.
> The bee is buzzing by
>   buttery treats!
> Please don't run. Eat your bun!

▶ Connect Sounds to Letters

Beginning Letter Display the *Benny Bear* card, and have children name the letter on the picture. Say: *The letter* b *stands for the sound / b /, as in* bear. *When you see a* b, *remember* Benny Bear. *That will help you remember the sound / b /.*

Write bear *on the board, underlining the* b. What is the first letter in the word *bear*? (b) **Bear** *starts with / b /, so* b *is the first letter I write for* bear.

Compare and Review: *t* In a pocket chart, display the *Benny Bear* card along with the Letter Cards *b* and *t*. Place the Picture Cards in random order. Review the sound for *t*. In turn, children name a picture, say the beginning sound, and put the card below the right letter.

Tell children they will sort more pictures in the Phonics Center today.

► Handwriting

Letter Cards B, b Tell children that they'll now learn to write the letters that stand for / b /: capital *B* and small *b*. Trace each letter as you recite the handwriting rhyme. Children can chant each rhyme as they "write" the letter in the air.

Handwriting Rhyme: B

Make a long line down.
Go back to the top.
Curve 'round
and 'round.

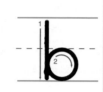

Handwriting Rhyme: b

Make a long line down.
A circle at the middle.
Nice and round.

► Apply

Practice Book page 87 Children will complete this page at small group time.

Blackline Master 158 This page provides additional handwriting practice.

At Group Time

Phonics Center

Use the Phonics Center materials for **Theme 3, Week 2, Day 2**.

Practice Book p. 87

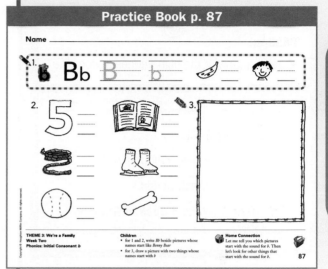

Name _____

THEME 3: We're a Family
Week Two
Phonics: Initial Consonant *b*

Children
• for 1 and 2, write *Bb* beside pictures whose names start like *Benny Bear*
• for 3, draw a picture with two things whose names start with *b*

Home Connection
Let me tell you which pictures start with the sound for *b*. Then let's look for other things that start with the sound for *b*.

87

Teacher's Note

Handwriting practice for the continuous stroke style is available on **Blackline Master 184**.

Portfolio Opportunity

Save the Practice Book page to show children's grasp of the letter-sound association.
Save **Blackline Master 158** for a handwriting sample.

✓High-Frequency Word

New Word: like

▶ Teach

Tell children that today they will learn to read and write a word that they will often see in stories. Say *like* and use it in context.

I *like* to sing. I *like* pizza. Do you *like* pizza?

Write *like* on the board, and have children spell it as you point to each letter. **Spell like *with me*, l-i-k-e.** Then lead children in a chant, clapping on each beat, to help them remember that *like* is spelled *l-i-k-e:* **l-i-k-e, like! l-i-k-e, like.**

Word Wall Ask children to help you decide where on the Word Wall *like* should be posted. As needed, prompt children by pointing out that like begins with the letter *l*. When children find the letter *l* on the Word Wall, add *like* beneath it. Remind children to look there when they need to remember how to write the word.

▶ Practice

Reading Build the following sentences in a pocket chart. Have children take turns reading the sentences aloud. Leave out the pocket chart so children can practice building and reading sentences.

Display *Higglety Pigglety: A Book of Rhymes,* page 6.

- Share the poem "Everybody Says" aloud.

- Reread the poem. *I'll read the poem one more time. This time, listen for the word* like. *If you hear it, raise your hand.*

- Call on children to point to the word *like* each time it appears in the poem.

THEME 1

Everybody Says

Everybody says
I look just like my mother.
Everybody says
I'm the image of Aunt Bee.
Everybody says
My nose is like my father's.
But I want to look like ME!

by Dorothy Aldis

6

Higglety Pigglety: A Book of Rhymes, page 6

▶ Apply

Practice Book page 88 Children will read and write *like* as they complete the Practice Book page.

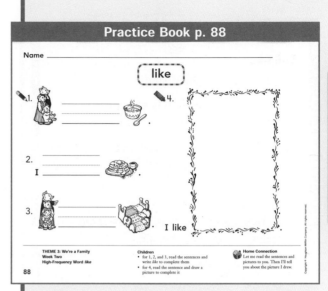

Practice Book p. 88

Diagnostic Check

If...	You can ...
children have problems writing or reading *like* on the Practice Book page,	have them build the word with block letters and use it in oral sentences.

OBJECTIVES

Children

- read high-frequency words
- create and write sentences with high-frequency words

MATERIALS

- **Word Cards** *I, like, my*
- **Picture Cards** *sandals, hat;* assorted others for sentence building
- **Punctuation Card:** period

High-Frequency Word Practice

▶ Building Sentences

Tell children that you want to build a sentence about favorite clothing.

■ Display the Word Cards and the Picture Cards *hat* and *sandals* in random order. Tell children that you will use these cards to build your sentence. Review the words together. Then explain that you are ready to build the sentence.

■ *I want the first word to be* I. *Who can find that word?*

■ Continue building the sentence until you have the stem *I like my* _____.

■ Explain that you want the next word in your sentence to name a kind of shoes. *Which picture should I choose?* Place the Picture Card *sandals* at the end of the sentence stem and add a period.

■ Read the completed sentence together, then continue with a new one.

Writing Opportunity Have children write and illustrate a sentence from the pocket chart. Have writers complete the sentence stem *I like my* _____ with their own rebus suggestions.

Vocabulary Expansion

▶ Types of Clothing

Remind children that in *Shoes From Grandpa* Jessie's family got together for a summer barbecue. Display pages 2–5 and have children review the pictures.

Viewing and Speaking Tell children that the clothes people choose to wear usually depend upon the time of year and the weather. Ask children to name the clothing Jessie's family is wearing. List their responses on chart paper.

■ Ask children to title the list, guiding them to suggest *Summer Clothes*. Then write the heading *Winter Clothes*. Ask: **What would people wear in the winter, when it is colder?** As needed, use the remaining story pictures as prompts.

Summer Clothes	Winter Clothes
shorts	pants
T-shirt	long-sleeved shirts
bathing suits	sweaters
sun dresses	coats, jackets
skirts	skirts

At Group Time
Art Center

(**Materials** • crayons or markers • Blackline Master 52)

Have children draw pictures of themselves doing a summer activity and pictures of themselves doing a winter activity. Ask children to share their drawings, commenting on the clothing worn in each.

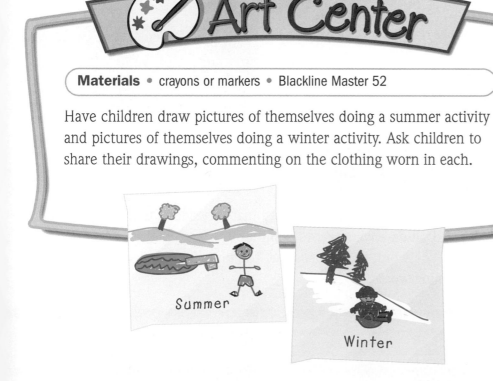

Challenge

MEETING INDIVIDUAL NEEDS

Some children may wish to brainstorm lists of clothing people might wear for various weather conditions, such as snow or rain. Children may also enjoy listing clothing and articles specific to different sports or activities.

Day 3

Opening

Day at a Glance

Learning to Read

Big Book:

Shoes From Grandpa

✓ **Phonics:**
Initial
Consonant *b*,
page T92

Word Work

Exploring Words, *page T94*

Writing & Language

Shared Writing, *page T95*

 Half-Day Kindergarten

✓ Indicates lessons for tested skills. Choose additional activities as time allows.

Calendar

Sunday	Monday	Tuesday	Wednesday	Thursday	Friday	Saturday
			1	2	3	4
5	6	7	8	9	10	11
12	13	14	15	16	17	18
19	20	21	22	23	24	25
26	27	28	29	30	31	

Continue to share some of the "news from home" during the calendar routine. Have children tell on which day of the week or on what date various events will or did take place.

Daily Message

Modeled Writing Incorporate class events into the daily message. Where appropriate, have children share the pen.

Today we will sort different types of clothes in the Math Center.

Ask children if they can find the word that they added to the Word Wall yesterday. Call on a volunteer to point it out. Have children chant the spelling of the word: **l-i-k-e** *spells* **like.** Continue in a similar manner with the remaining words.

✓ Daily Phonemic Awareness
Beginning Sounds

- *Let's listen for beginning sounds. I will say two words, you tell me which word begins with Benny Bear's sound, /b/. Listen:* big, little.

- *Say the words with me:* big, little. *Which word begins with /b/?... Yes, big begins with /b/.*

- Continue with the words shown.

boy/girl   cook/bus
bath/top   sand/buy
back/fork   good/bear
car/bake   bug/sweet

Getting Ready to Learn

To help plan their day, tell children that they will

- reread and talk about the Big Book: *Shoes From Grandpa*.

- read a story called "Baby Bear's Family."

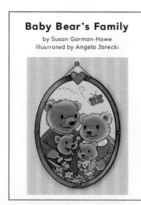

- categorize clothes in the Math Center.

Summer   Winter

DAY 3

Day 3

Sharing the Big Book

Children

• draw conclusions

• recognize use of capital letter at the beginning of a sentence

• recognize use of end punctuation

• observe use of directionality: return sweep

Big Book

Reading SHOES FROM GRANDPA
by MEM FOX • Illustrated by PATRICIA MULLINS

Includes:
Social Studies Link

Reading for Understanding Reread the story, noting the language pattern. Pause for Supporting Comprehension points.

Extra Support

Point out details in the pictures to help children grasp the switch between the summer barbecue to Jessie's visions of her family's winter gifts.

LATE one summer Jessie's father invited all the family over for a barbecue.

pages 2–3

When Grandpa saw Jessie he stood back and said, "My, how you've grown! You'll need a new pair of shoes this winter, and I'll buy them."

pages 4–5

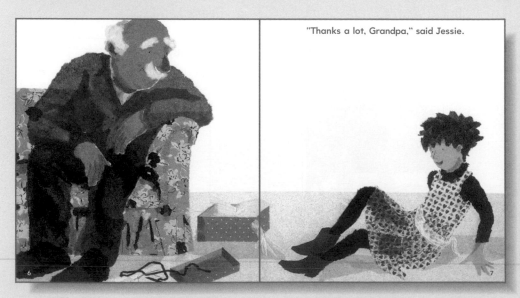

"Thanks a lot, Grandpa," said Jessie.

pages 6–7

Then her dad said,
"I'll buy you some socks from the local shops,
to go with the shoes from Grandpa."

pages 8–9

And her mom said,
"I'll buy you a skirt that won't show the dirt,
to go with the socks from the local shops,
to go with the shoes from Grandpa."

pages 10–11

And her cousin said,
"I'll look for a blouse with ribbons and bows,
to go with the skirt that won't show the dirt,
to go with the socks from the local shops,
to go with the shoes from Grandpa."

pages 12–13

▶ Supporting Comprehension

title page
Strategy: Predict/Infer

Teacher-Student Modeling Review how you made predictions before reading yesterday. Prompts: *What did the title and the pictures tell us about the story? Was the man on the cover Grandpa? Were the other people in the picture the girl's (Jessie's) family?*

pages 4–5
Noting Details

- *Why did Grandpa say he'd buy Jessie new shoes?* (She had grown.)

pages 6–11
Evaluate

- *Do you think it is winter already or do you think Jessie is imagining what her family's gifts will look like? Why do you think that?*

Revisiting the Text

pages 4–5
Concepts of Print

☑ **Capitalize First Word in Sentence; End Punctuation**

- Remind children that every sentence begins and ends in a certain way. *How does each sentence begin? How does each sentence end?* Help children identify the beginning and end of each sentence on the page.

DAY 3

▶ **Supporting Comprehension**

pages 14–15

✓ **Comprehension Focus:**
   Inferences: Drawing Conclusions

Teacher-Student Modeling *Good readers use clues to make decisions about a story. Use story and picture clues to tell me who the girl is with Jessie.* (Jessie's sister) *Do you think Jessie likes the sweater? Why or why not?*

pages 16–19

Strategy: Predict/Infer

Student Modeling After reading page 17 ask: *What do you think will happen next? Why do you say that?* (Another family member will offer Jessie a gift; that's the story pattern.) Read pages 18–19 to confirm children's predictions.

pages 18–19

Evaluate

■ *Do you agree with Jessie's aunt? Is she making a scarf that will make people laugh? Why?*

And her sister said,
"I'll get you a sweater
   when the weather gets wetter,
to go with the blouse with ribbons and bows,
to go with the skirt that won't show the dirt,
to go with the socks from the local shops,
to go with the shoes from Grandpa."

pages 14–15

And her grandma said,
"I'll find you a coat you could wear on a boat,
to go with the sweater
   when the weather gets wetter,
to go with the blouse with ribbons and bows,
to go with the skirt that won't show the dirt,
to go with the socks from the local shops,
to go with the shoes from Grandpa."

pages 16–17

And her aunt said,
"I'll knit you a scarf that'll make us all laugh,
to go with the coat you could wear on a boat,
to go with the sweater
   when the weather gets wetter,
to go with the blouse with ribbons and bows,

pages 18–19

"to go with the skirt that won't show the dirt,
to go with the socks from the local shops,
to go with the shoes from Grandpa."

20   21

pages 20–21

And her brother said,
"I'll find you a hat you can put on like that,
to go with the scarf that'll make us all laugh,
to go with the coat you could wear on a boat,
to go with the sweater
    when the weather gets wetter,

to go with the blouse with ribbons and bows,
to go with the skirt that won't show the dirt,
to go with the socks from the local shops,
to go with the shoes from Grandpa."

22   23

pages 22–23

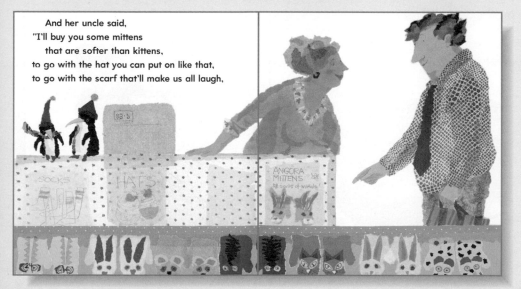

And her uncle said,
"I'll buy you some mittens
    that are softer than kittens,
to go with the hat you can put on like that,
to go with the scarf that'll make us all laugh,

pages 24–25

▶ Supporting Comprehension

pages 22–23

☑ **Comprehension Focus: Inferences: Drawing Conclusions**

Student Modeling *Use story and picture clues to tell me about Jessie's brother. What does he like to do? Do you think it would be fun to have Jessie's brother as a friend? Why or why not?*

pages 24–25

Evaluate

■ *Which mittens would you choose? Why?*

Revisiting the Text

pages 22–23

Concepts of Print

☑ **Return Sweep; End Punctuation**

■ Read page 22, tracking the print with your hand. Point out that when you reach the end of the line, you *return* to the beginning of the next line to read.

■ Frame the first word on page 22 and read it. *And begins with a capital letter; it is the first word in the sentence. The marks in the sentence tell us to pause, but they are not end marks. I'll keep reading and you tell me when you see the end of the sentence.* Point out that the sentence is so long that it doesn't end until page 23.

DAY 3

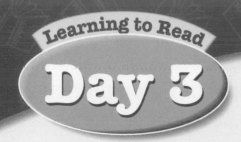
▶ **Supporting Comprehension**

pages 26–27
Story Structure: Characters

■ *How do you think Jessie is feeling?*

pages 26–27

- -

pages 28–29

✓ **Comprehension Focus:**
Inferences: Drawing Conclusions

Student Modeling *What kind of person do you think Jessie is? Why does she say she "hates to be mean" when she asks for someone to buy her some jeans?* (Jessie is nice; she doesn't want to hurt anyone's feelings, but she also wants a pair of jeans.)

- -

pages 28–29

pages 30–31
Evaluate

■ *Did someone buy Jessie's jeans? Why do you say that? When do you think Jessie got her jeans—in the summer or in the winter?*

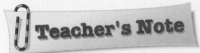
Teacher's Note

Language Patterns
The cumulative text and the use of rhyming pairs within many of the sentences creates a strong pattern that many children will notice. As you reread the story, pause for children to join in on repeated lines and rhyming words.

pages 30–31

In the story excerpt:

"to go with the coat you could wear on a boat,
to go with the sweater
   when the weather gets wetter,
to go with the blouse with ribbons and bows,
to go with the skirt that won't show the dirt,
to go with the socks from the local shops,
to go with the shoes from Grandpa."

   And Jessie said,
"You're all so kind that I hate to be mean,
but please, would one of you buy me some jeans?"

page 32

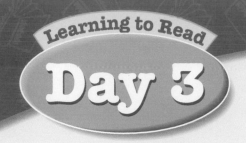
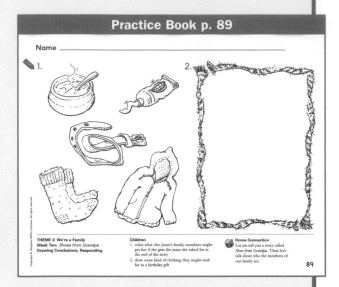

▶ Responding to the Story

Retelling Use these prompts to help children summarize *Shoes from Grandpa*

- *Why does Grandpa offer to buy Jessie shoes?*

- *What does each family member then offer to do?*

- *How are all the gifts the same? How are they different?* (All of the gifts were articles of clothing; all are different articles.)

- *What did you like best about the story? Why?*

Practice Book page 89 Children will complete the page at small group time.

At Group Time

+= Math Center

Materials • magazines and catalogs • drawing paper • scissors • glue

Children choose they type of weather the would like to find pictures of clothing for: *Summer* and *Winter,* or *Rainy* and *Snowy.* Children find and cut out pictures of clothing to sort and paste under the appropriate headings.

At Group Time

Art Center

Materials • crayons or markers • drawing paper

Remind children that Jessie's favorite present is a pair of jeans. Children draw their favorite present and write a label for their picture. Then children can share their drawings with a friend.

red bike

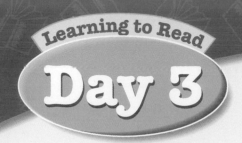
 Extra Support

Read "Baa, Baa, Black Sheep," *Higglety Pigglety: A Book of Rhymes* page 16. Have children "bob" their heads each time they hear a word that begins with / b /. Then call on volunteers to point to words that begin with *b* in the rhyme.

Phonics

Initial Consonant b

▶ Connect Sounds to Letters

Read the lyrics to Benny Bear's song, and have children listen for the / b / words. *If you hear a word that begins with / b / stand up. If you hear another / b / word, sit back down. We'll do this each time we hear a / b / word.* As needed, model standing and sitting alternately for / b / words as you read the first line. Then say the entire song, having just children stand and sit for / b / words.

> **Benny Bear's Song**
> (Tune: "Three Blind Mice")
> Benny Bear, Benny Bear.
> Please beware! Please beware!
> I see a bee near the basket
>   of beets.
> The bee is buzzing by
>   buttery treats!
> Please don't run. Eat your bun!

▶ Connect Sounds to Letters

Beginning Letter *b* Display the *Benny Bear* card and have children name the letter on the picture. *What letter stands for the sound / b /, as in* bear? (*b*) *Who can help you remember the sound / b /?* (Benny Bear)

Write *bear* on the board, underlining the *b*. *What is the first letter in the word* bear? Bear *starts with / b /, so* b *is the first letter I write for* bear.

Compare and Review Display the Letter Cards *b* and *t* on the chalkboard ledge. Review the sound for *t* with children. Then distribute Picture Cards for *b* and *t,* one to a child, to a group of children. In turn, children name the picture, say the beginning sound, and stand by the correct letter on the chalkboard ledge. Children without Picture Cards verify their decisions.

Repeat the activity with different groups of children until each child has a chance to name a picture, say the beginning sound, and stand beside the letter on the chalkboard ledge.

Phonics in Action

We're a Family

Applying Skills

▶ Introducing the Story

Let's read the title. It says "Baby Bear's Family." I see four bears on the title page. Do you think this is baby bear's family? Which one do you think is baby bear?

Together identify pictures that begin with the /b/ sound on the title page.

Let's look at the pictures to see what the story is about. As you do a picture walk, guide children in a discussion of the pictures.

▶ Coached Reading

Have children carefully look at each page before reading with you. Prompts:

page 10   *What is the Mama Bear doing? What are Baby Bear and his brother doing?*

page 11   *Where is the family? What is Papa Bear doing? Where is Baby Bear going?*

pages 12-13 *What is Baby Bear doing? Does the rest of his family know where he is?*

page 15   *Where is the family now? What is everyone doing?*

Now let's go back and look at each page to find things that begin with Benny Bear's sound /b/.

Phonics Library

Purposes
- read a wordless story
- find pictures beginning with /b/

Baby Bear's Family
by Susan Gorman-Howe
illustrated by Angela Jarecki

9

10   11

12   13

14   15

DAY 3

Home Connection

Children can color the pictures in the take-home version of "Baby Bear's Family." After rereading on Day 4, children can take it home to read to family members.

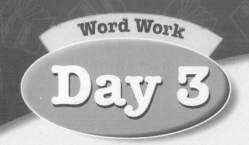

Exploring Words

▶ Family Words

Read aloud "Everybody Says" on page 6 of *Higglety Pigglety: A Book of Rhymes.* Remind children that they have been talking about families and words that name family members. As you read the poem again, ask children to raise their hands when they hear a word that names a family member. (*mother, aunt, father*)

■ Review the words on the People in a Family chart. Help children find the words *mother, aunt,* and *father.*

■ Point out that resemblances can be shared mannerisms or favorite activities. Ask: *Do you resemble a family member or friend? How?* Model for children a possible response by sharing your own likenesses, for example: *I like to cook like my father.*

■ Encourage children to share responses with the class.

Writing Opportunity Have children draw pictures of family members or friends they resemble in some way. Children dictate a label for their pictures. Provide time for children to share their pictures and tell about them.

Shared Writing

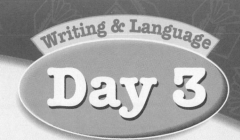
▶ Writing a Grocery List

Listening and Speaking Recall with children why Jessie's family had gathered together. (for a barbecue) Have children share what they know about barbecues.

■ *How do you think Jessie's family got ready for the barbecue? Do you think they went grocery shopping? What kinds of things do you think they needed to buy?*

■ Explain that when people have to buy many things, like groceries, they often make a shopping list. Ask if children have ever helped their parents make a shopping list before going to the grocery store. Then suggest that children help you make a shopping list for a family barbecue.

Review the pictures on pages 2–5 of *Shoes From Grandpa*. Tell children that they can use clues in the pictures along with what they already know about barbecues to help you make the shopping list.

■ Brainstorm with children a list of items they would buy for a barbecue.

■ After the list is complete, ask children to help you think of a good title, and record it at the top of the list.

OBJECTIVES

Children
• write a grocery list

MATERIALS

• **Big Book:** *Shoes from Grandpa*

English Language Learners

Teach vocabulary related to food. Use magazine photos or grocery store ads and have children cut out pictures of food to make a "picture" grocery list. Have them share their lists orally with the rest of the class. Assist with vocabulary.

DAY 3

Day 4

Day at a Glance

Learning to Read

Big Book:

Which Would You Choose?

 Phonics: Review Initial Consonant *b*, page T100

Word Work

Exploring Words, *page T102*

Writing & Language

Interactive Writing, *page T103*

 Half-Day Kindergarten

 Indicates lessons for tested skills. Choose additional activities as time allows.

Opening

....

Calendar

Sunday	Monday	Tuesday	Wednesday	Thursday	Friday	Saturday
			1	2	3	4
5	6	7	8	9	10	11
12	13	14	15	16	17	18
19	20	21	22	23	24	25
26	27	28	29	30	31	

Continue to incorporate family words and activities into the calendar routine. *Let's make Thursday night Share a Book Night. Remember to share your take-home story with a family member.*

....

Daily Message

Modeled Writing Use some words that begin with *b* in today's message. Call on volunteers to circle the *b*'s.

We go to the library today. We will take out new books.

Read the Word Wall together, then play a rhyming game: *I'm going to find a word on the wall that rhymes with fly. Fly rhymes with... my. Raise your hand when you find a word that rhymes with bike.* (*like*)

Daily Phonemic Awareness
Beginning Sounds

- *Listen as I say two words:* bike, ball. *Say the words with me:* bike, ball. *Do you hear the same sound at the beginning of each word?... Yes,* bike *and* ball *begin with the same sound. Help children isolate the beginning sound,* /b/.

- Invite children to play What's the Sound? with children. Explain that you will say two words that begin with the same sound. They should raise their hands when they know the sound.

- Say the following pairs of words. For each pair, have children isolate and identify the beginning sound.

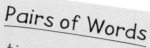

Pairs of Words

tiger/turkey
mittens/muffins
banana/boy
balloon/butter
raison/red
table/telephone
pencil/penny
summer/sunny

Getting Ready to Learn

To help plan their day, tell children that they will

- read the Social Studies Link: *Which Would You Choose?*

- sort words that begin with *b* in the Phonics Center.

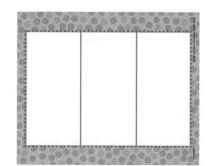

- reread a story called "Baby Bear's Family."

DAY 4

Big Book

pages 33–39

Sharing the Big Book
Social Studies Link

▶ **Building Background**

Read aloud the title and discuss the cover photograph. Ask children when they might choose to wear the pictured items.

Reading for Understanding Pause for discussion as you share the selection.

page 33

Strategy: Predict/Infer

Page through the selection, allowing children to look at the pictures.

Student Modeling Remind children that often good readers can predict what a story is about by looking at the pictures. *What do you think this selection is about? Why do you think that?*

pages 34–35

Comprehension Focus:
Inferences: Drawing Conclusions

Student Modeling *What does mom love to do? What clues tell you this? What gloves should she choose to work in the garden? How does what you already know about gloves help you pick the right ones?*

page 36
Evaluate

■ *Why will a sweater make this father feel better?* (He's cold; the sweater will make him feel warmer.)

page 37
Noting Details

■ *At what time of year would you wear a T-shirt and shorts? At what time of year would you wear a sweater like this?*

pages 38–39
Compare and Contrast

■ *Which gloves would the girl wear to play in the snow? to play baseball? How are the gloves alike? How are they different? Which shoes would she wear to run and play? to jump in puddles? How do these shoes compare?*

Mom needs her gloves
to do something she loves.

Which should she choose?

34

35

pages 34–35

Dad needs his sweater
to make him feel better.

Which should he choose?

36

37

pages 36–37

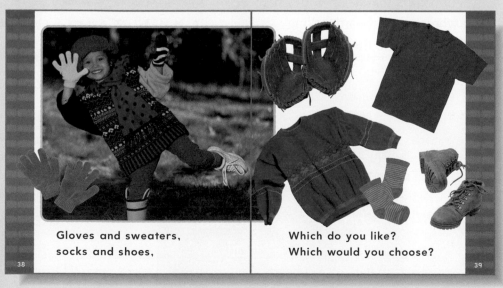

Gloves and sweaters,
socks and shoes,

Which do you like?
Which would you choose?

38

39

pages 38–39

Revisiting the Text

pages 36–37

Concepts of Print

✓ **Capitalize First Word in Sentence; End Punctuation; Return Sweep**

■ Ask a volunteer to track the print as you read the sentence on page 36. Point out that when the child came to the end of a line, he or she returned to the beginning of the next line to keep reading.

■ Have another child find the first word in the sentence and identify the capital *M*. Call on a third child to find and identify the end punctuation.

■ Repeat with the sentence on page 37.

▶ Responding

Summarizing Allow children to respond to the questions at the end of the selection. Then have children summarize the selection, using the pictures as prompts.

Extra Support

Examine each picture with children. If children are unsure as to which item to choose, help them eliminate unlikely choices first.

Challenge

For children who are ready for a challenge, prepare cards for the words and end marks in one or two sentences from the selection. One child builds a sentence and reads it with a partner.

Sharing the Big Book T99

DAY 4

Phonics

✓ Review Initial Consonant b

MATERIALS

- **Alphafriend Cards** *Benny Bear, Mimi Mouse, Reggie Rooster*
- **Alphafolder** *Benny Bear*
- **Letter Cards** *b, m, r*
- **Picture Cards** for *b, m, r*
- ***From Apples to Zebras: A Book of ABC's,*** page 3
- **Phonics Center:** Theme 3, Week 2, Day 4

▶ Phonemic Awareness

Beginning Sound Display the scene in Benny Bear's Alphafolder. *One thing I see is a buzzing bee. Say* bee *with me. Does* bee *begin with the same sound as Benny Bear, /b/?* Call on volunteers to point to and name other items in the picture that begin with /b/.

▶ Connect Sounds to Letters

Review Consonant *b* Using self-stick notes, cover the words on page 3 of *From Apples to Zebras: A Book of ABC's.* Then display the page. Ask children what letter they expect to see first in each word and why. Uncover the words so that children can check their predictions.

Have children look around the room and list names of objects that begin with /b/. Write the words on the board, asking volunteers to underline the *b* in each word you write.

From Apples to Zebras: A Book of ABC's, page 3

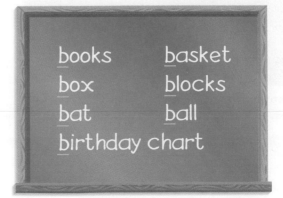

books   basket
box   blocks
bat   ball
birthday chart

Home Connection

Challenge children to look at home for items or for names that begin with the consonant *b*. Children can draw pictures to show what they have found.

▶ Apply

Compare and Review: *r, m* In a pocket chart, display the card for *Benny Bear* and the Letter Cards *b, r,* and *m.* Review the sound for *r,* /r/, and *m,* /m/. Place the Picture Cards in the pocket chart in random order. Ask children to name a picture, say the beginning sound, and place the card below the right letter.

Pictures: *bed, rope, map, boat, rake, red, mix, bike, man*

Tell children they will sort more pictures in the Phonics Center today.

Practice Book page 90 Children will complete this page at small group time.

Phonics Library In groups today, children will also identify *b* words as they reread the **Phonics Library** story "Baby Bear's Family." See suggestions, page T93.

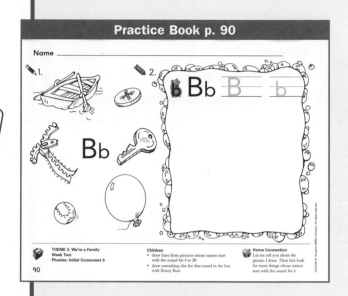

Phonics Center

Use the Phonics Center materials for **Theme 3, Week 2, Day 4**.

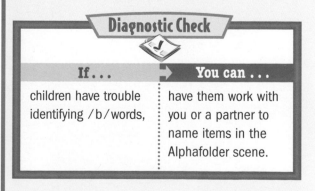

DAY 4

Diagnostic Check

If . . .	You can . . .
children have trouble identifying /b/ words,	have them work with you or a partner to name items in the Alphafolder scene.

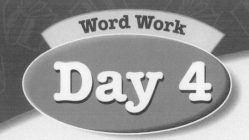

Day 4

Children

• explore family words

Exploring Words

▶ Family Words

Display the People in a Family Chart created last week. (See page T38.) Read through the chart with children.

■ Recall that in the selection *Which Would You Choose?* there was a mother, a father, and a girl—their daughter. Help children find the words *mother, father,* and *daughter* on the chart.

■ Review the family chores completed in the story. ***What chores do you do to help at home? Do you do the chores alone or do you do them with another family member?***

■ List children's suggestions on chart paper.

How I Help at Home

make my bed
take out the trash
set the table
pick up toys

Writing Opportunity Have children draw a picture to show what they do at home to help. Children can draw a chore that they do alone or one that they do with someone else. Children can label their pictures by writing what chore it is or by naming the people that do the chore.

me   Dad

Interactive Writing

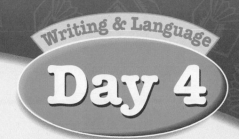

▶ Choosing a Good Title

Speaking Remind children that yesterday they made a shopping list of things they would need for a family barbecue.

Display the chart from yesterday's shared writing, and review the items that children recorded.

- ■ Brainstorm additional items to add to the chart. Prompt children as needed: *I see that we have hot dogs and hamburgers to eat, but I don't see a dessert. What would be a good dessert for a barbecue? We have paper plates and cups on our list, but we don't have any forks or knives. What do we need to eat the potato salad?*

- ■ Continue reviewing the list, calling on children to contribute items. Have children share in the writing where appropriate.

- ■ Read the title again. *Should we change the title any way? Do you think we should be more specific? Yes, the word **barbecue** should be a part of the title.* Entertain children's ideas, and alter the title of the grocery list as suggested.

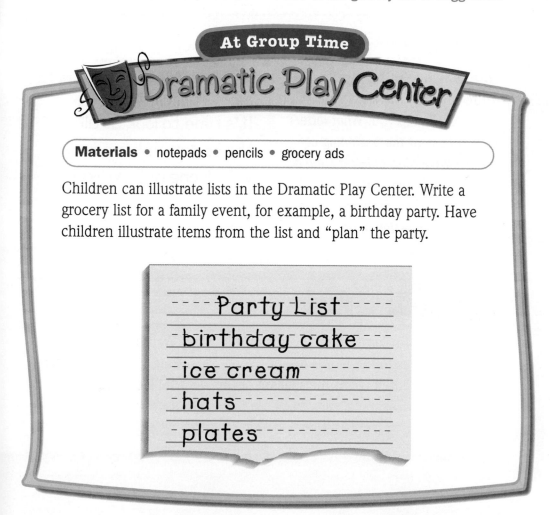

At Group Time

Dramatic Play Center

| Materials • notepads • pencils • grocery ads |

Children can illustrate lists in the Dramatic Play Center. Write a grocery list for a family event, for example, a birthday party. Have children illustrate items from the list and "plan" the party.

```
Party List
birthday cake
ice cream
hats
plates
```

Learning to Read
Day 5

Day at a Glance

Learning to Read

Revisiting the Literature:

Goldilocks and the Three Bears, Shoes From Grandpa, Which Would You Choose?, "Baby Bear's Family"

☑ **Phonics Review: Initial Consonants b, m, r, t** page T108

Word Work

Exploring Words, *page T110*

Writing & Language

Independent Writing, *page T111*

☀ **Half-Day Kindergarten**

☑ Indicates lessons for tested skills. Choose additional activities as time allows.

Opening

Calendar

Sunday	Monday	Tuesday	Wednesday	Thursday	Friday	Saturday
			1	2	3	4
5	6	7	8	9	10	11
12	13	14	15	16	17	18
19	20	21	22	23	24	25
26	27	28	29	30	31	

Discuss children's weekend plans with the class. *Will you and your family do chores this weekend? Will you have some fun, too? Do you think you will read together?*

Daily Message

Interactive Writing As you write the daily message, call on children to help you. *What letter should I use at the beginning of books? What kind of letter should I use to begin the sentence? Should I end the sentence with a period or a question mark?*

It's time to look at all the books we have read. Which one did you like?

Distribute Word Cards for the words on the Word Wall. Have children match the cards to the words on the Word Wall. After a match is made, have other children chant the spelling of the word: l-i-k-e *spells* like.

Routines

Daily Phonemic Awareness
Beginning Sounds

- Play Same Sound Sort with children.

- *I will say two words. Listen carefully to find out if the two words begin with the same sound.*

- Remind children that if the words begin with the same sound, they should raise their hands. If the words do not begin with the same sound, they should cover their ears.

- Use the words shown here.

boat/book	car/man
robot/rain	fish/feather
rain/room	hand/hammer
bugs/beach	boxes/carts

Getting Ready to Learn

To help plan their day, tell children that they will

- reread and talk about all the books they've read this week.

- take home a story they can read.

Baby Bear's Family
by Susan Gorman-Howe
illustrated by Angela Jarecki

- write in their journals.

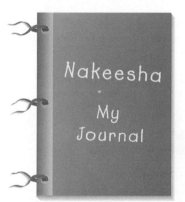

Nakeesha
My
Journal

DAY 5

Revisiting the Literature

⋯⋯⋯⋯⋯⋯⋯⋯⋯⋯⋯⋯⋯⋯⋯⋯⋯⋯⋯

▶ Literature Discussion

Today children compare the different books you shared this week: *Goldilocks and the Three Bears, Shoes From Grandpa, Which Would You Choose?*, and "Baby Bear's Family." Use these suggestions to help children recall the selections:

■ Ask children to retell *Goldilocks and the Three Bears*. Have them restate the lesson Goldilocks learned.

■ Display *Shoes From Grandpa*. Ask children what Jessie's family members promised to do. Then ask what article of clothing Jessie really wanted.

■ Have children recall *Which Would You Choose?* Call on volunteers to tell how people choose to wear different clothes.

■ Together, reread "Baby Bear's Family." Ask volunteers to name the /b/ pictures in the story.

■ Ask children to vote for their favorite book of the week. Then read the text of the winner aloud.

 Comprehension Focus:
Inferences: Drawing Conclusions

Comparing Books Remind children that good readers use story and picture clues to make decisions about a story. Display each selection and have children recall decisions they made about the story. Children might, for example, recall drawing conclusions about what the three bears would find when they returned home. They may recall conclusions they drew about Jessie's family in *Shoes From Grandpa* or the decisions they made about the clothing needed by the characters in *Which Would You Choose?*

www.eduplace.com
Log on to **Education Place** for more activities relating to We're a Family.

www.bookadventure.org
This Internet reading-incentive program provides thousands of titles for children to read.

Building Fluency

▶ Rereading Familiar Texts

Phonics Library:"Baby Bear's Family" Remind children that they've learned the new word *like*, and that they've been learning about words with initial *b*/b/. As they reread the **Phonics Library** stories "Baby Bear's Family" and "The Birthday Party," have them look for /b/ pictures.

Review Feature several familiar **Phonics Library** titles in the Book Corner. Have children demonstrate their growing skills by choosing one to reread aloud, alternating pages with a partner. From time to time ask children to point out words or pages that they can read more easily now.

Oral Reading Long before children begin formal reading, they often develop a good sense of story and story language. Wordless stories can help you assess this ability. As you read together, monitor how skillfully children interpret illustrations. Do they have a sense of story structure? Do they independently use "story language" such as *Once upon a time*?

Baby Bear's Family
by Susan Gorman-Howe
illustrated by Angela Jarecki

We Go to School
by Susan Gorman-Howe
illustrated by Maryann Cocca-Leffler

The Birthday Party
by Susan Gorman-Howe
illustrated by Grace Lin

Blackline Master 36 Children complete the page and take it home to share their reading progress.

My Reading Log

I can read.

My new word
-------- like --------

Leveled Books

The materials listed below provide reading practice for children at different levels.

Little Big Books

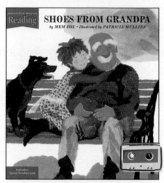

Little Readers for Guided Reading

Houghton Mifflin Classroom Bookshelf

Home Connection

Remind children to share the take-home version of "Baby Bear's Family" with their families.

DAY 5

Phonics Review
✔️ *Initial Consonants b, m, r, t*

▶ Review

Tell children that they will take turns naming pictures and telling what letter stands for the beginning sound.

- ■ Randomly place four picture cards along the chalkboard ledge and write *b, m, r,* and *t* on the board. Call on four children to stand in front of a picture. Have each child name the picture, isolate the initial sound, and point to the beginning consonant on the board.

- ■ The rest of the class can verify that the correct letter has been chosen. Then write the picture name on the board and underline the initial consonant.

- ■ Continue until everyone has a chance to name a picture and point to the initial consonant.

High-Frequency Word Review
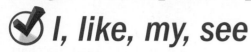 *I, like, my, see*

▶ Review

Give each small group the Word Cards, Picture Cards, and Punctuation Card needed to make a sentence. Each child holds one card. Children stand and arrange themselves to make a sentence for others to read.

▶ Apply

Practice Book page 91 Children can complete this page independently and read it to you during small group time.

Phonics Library Have children take turns reading aloud to the class. Each child might read one page of "Baby Bear's Family" or a favorite Phonics Library selection from the previous theme. Remind readers to share the pictures! Discussion questions:

■ *Find a picture that starts with the same sound as Benny Bear's name. What is the letter? What is the sound?*

■ *Let's look at the title page of "My Red Boat." Can you find the letter with the /b/ sound? Do you see any pictures that begin with /b/?*

Practice Book p. 91

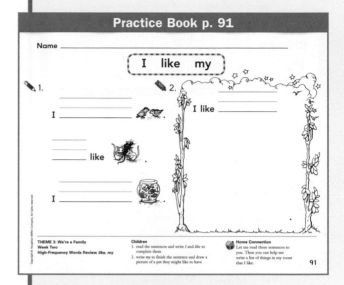

Portfolio Opportunity
Save the Practice Book page to show children's recognition of high-frequency words.

Diagnostic Check

If . . .	You can . . .
children need help remembering the sound for consonant *b*,	have them listen to Benny Bear's song and listen for *b* words.

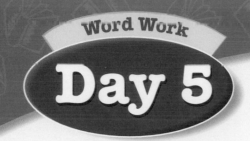
OBJECTIVES

Children

• explore family words

Exploring Words

....

▶ Family Words

Direct attention to the People in a Family Chart. (See page T38.) Read the chart with children.

■ Point out to children that many of them enjoy playing "house" in the Dramatic Play Center. Ask children to tell what roles they like to play and why.

Writing Opportunity Provide partners with an index card. Assign a family name for each pair to write on the index card. Help children punch holes in the cards and tie a length of string to them. Place the name tags in the Dramatic Play Center for children to wear while role playing family settings.

Independent Writing

▶ Journals

Tell children that today they will write in their journals.

- Pass out the journals.

- Recall *Shoes From Grandpa*. **What were some of the things that Jessie's family said they would buy her in the winter? What did Jessie really want?**

- Remind children that they made a list for the barbecue. Ask them to think about the reasons people make lists. Then suggest that they write their own lists for things *they* will need this winter.

- Tell children that they can draw their lists and use the words on the Word Wall and in the Writing Center to help them as they write. Children can also browse through this week's literature for ideas.

- If time permits, have children share what they've written with the class.

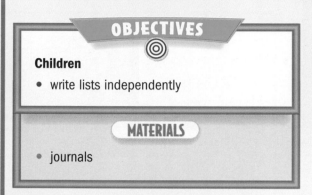

OBJECTIVES

Children
- write lists independently

MATERIALS

- journals

Portfolio Opportunity

Mark journal entries you would like to share with parents. Allow children to mark their best efforts or favorite works for sharing as well.

DAY 5

Literature for Week 3
Different texts for different purposes

Teacher Read Alouds:
- **Jonathan and His Mommy**
- **Goldilocks and the Three Bears**
- **The Amazing Little Porridge Pot**

Purposes
- oral language
- listening strategy
- comprehension skill

Big Books:

Higglety Pigglety: A Book of Rhymes

Purposes
- oral language development
- phonemic awareness

From Apples to Zebras: A Book of ABC's

Purposes
- alphabet recognition
- letters and sounds

Big Books: Main Selections
Purposes
- concepts of print
- reading strategy
- story language
- comprehension skills

Also available in Little Big Book and audiotape

Also available in Little Big Book and audiotape

Leveled Books

Also in the Big Books:
- Social Studies Links

Purposes

- reading strategies
- comprehension skills
- concepts of print

Phonics Library

Also available in Take-Home version

Purpose

- applying phonics skills and high-frequency words

On My Way Paperback

On My Way
Practice Readers

Nicky Takes a Bath
by Sam Fonte
page T157

Little Readers for Guided Reading
Collection K

Houghton Mifflin Classroom Bookshelf
Level K

Technology

www.eduplace.com
Log on to *Education Place* for more activities relating to *We're a Family*.

www.bookadventure.org
This free Internet reading incentive program provides thousands of titles for students to read.

Suggested Daily Routines

Instructional Goals

Learning to Read

✓ *Phonemic Awareness:* Beginning Sounds

Strategy Focus: Summarize, Evaluate

✓ *Comprehension Skill:* Inferences: Drawing Conclusions, Story Structure: Characters/Setting

✓ *Phonics Skills*

Phonemic Awareness: Beginning Sound /n/ Initial Consonant *N, n*

Compare and Review: Initial Consonants: *b, t*

✓ *High-Frequency Review Words:* my, like

✓ *Concepts of Print:* Capital at Beginning of Sentence, End Punctuation; Return Sweep

Word Work

High-Frequency Word Practice: Building Sentences, Environmental Print

Writing & Language

Vocabulary Skills: Using Action Words, Using Order Words

Writing Skill: Using Order Words

✓ = tested skills

 Leveled Books

Have children read in appropriate levels daily.

Phonics Library
On My Way Practice Readers
Little Big Books
Houghton Mifflin Classroom Bookshelf

Day 1

Opening Routines, *T118–T119*

[Word | Wall]

• **Phonemic Awareness:** Beginning Sounds

Teacher Read Aloud
The Amazing Little Porridge Pot, T120–T123
• **Strategy:** Summarize
• **Comprehension:** Inferences: Drawing Conclusions

Phonics

Instruction
• Phonemic Awareness, Beginning Sound /n/, T124–T125; *Practice Book, 95–96*

High-Frequency Word Practice
• Words: *I, like, my, see, T126*

Oral Language
• Using Action Words, *T127*

Managing Small Groups
Teacher-Led Group
• Reread familiar **Phonics Library** selections

Independent Groups
• Finish *Practice Book, 93–96*
• *Phonics Center:* Theme 3, Week 3, Day 1
• Dramatic Play, Writing, other Centers

Day 2

Opening Routines, *T128–T129*

[Word | Wall]

• **Phonemic Awareness:** Beginning Sounds

Sharing the Big Book
Tortillas and Lullabies, T130–T131
• **Strategy:** Summarize
• **Comprehension:** Inferences: Story Structure: Characters/Setting

Phonics

Instruction, Practice
• Initial Consonant *n, T132–T133*
• *Practice Book, 98*

High-Frequency Words
• Review Words: *my, like, T134–T135*
• *Practice Book, 99*

High-Frequency Word Practice
• Building Sentences, *T136*

Vocabulary Expansion
• Using Order Words, *T137*
• Viewing and Speaking, *T137*

Managing Small Groups
Teacher-Led Group
• Begin *Practice Book, 97–99* and handwriting Blackline Masters **170** or **196.**

Independent Groups
• Finish *Practice Book, 97–99* and handwriting Blackline Masters **170** or **196.**
• *Phonics Center:* Theme 3, Week 3, Day 2
• Math, Art, other Centers

Technology

Lesson Planner CD-ROM: Customize your planning for *We're Family* with the Lesson Planner.

Day 3

Opening Routines, *T138–T139*

[Word Wall]

- **Phonemic Awareness:** Beginning Sounds

Sharing the Big Book
Shoes From Grandpa, T140–T141
- **Strategy:** Summarize
- **Comprehension:** Inferences: Drawing Conclusions, *T140*

Phonics
Practice, Application
- Initial Consonant *n*, *T142–T143*

Instruction
- Beginning Letter *n*, *T142–T143*
- **Phonics Library:** "Cat's Surprise," *T143*

Exploring Words
- Environmental Print, *T144*

✎ **Shared Writing**
- Using Order Words, *T145*
- Listening and Speaking, *T145*

Managing Small Groups
Teacher-Led Group
- Read **Phonics Library** selection "Cat's Surprise"
- Begin *Practice Book, 100*

Independent Groups
- Finish *Practice Book, 100*
- Science, other Centers

Day 4

Opening Routines, *T146–T147*

[Word Wall]

- **Phonemic Awareness:** Beginning Sounds

Sharing the Big Book
Social Studies Links: "Families," "Which Would You Choose?" *T148–T149*
- **Strategy:** Evaluate, Predict/Infer
- **Comprehension:** Drawing Conclusions
- **Concepts of Print:** Capital at Beginning of Sentence; End Punctuation; Return Sweep

Phonics
Practice
- Review Initial Consonant *n*, *T150–T151*; *Practice Book, 101*

Exploring Words
- Environmental Print, *T152*

✎ **Interactive Writing**
- Using Order Words, *T153*
- Speaking, *T153*

Managing Small Groups
Teacher-Led Group
- Reread **Phonics Library** selection "Cat's Surprise"
- Begin *Practice Book, 101*

Independent Groups
- Finish *Practice Book, 101*
- *Phonics Center:* Theme 3, Week 3, Day 4
- Art, other Centers

Day 5

Opening Routines, *T154–T155*

[Word Wall]

- **Phonemic Awareness:** Beginning Sounds

Revisiting the Literature
Comprehension: Characters/Setting, Drawing Conclusions, *T156*
Building Fluency
- **On My Way Practice Reader:** "Nicky Takes a Bath," *T157*

Phonics
Review
- Initial Consonants: *b, m, n, r, s, t, T158*

High-Frequency Word Review
- Words: *I, see, my, like, T159*; *Practice Book, 102*

Exploring Words
- Environmental Print, *T160*

✎ **Independent Writing**
- Journals: About Family, *T161*

Managing Small Groups
Teacher-Led Group
- Reread familiar **Phonics Library** selections
- Begin *Practice Book, 102,* Blackline Master 36.

Independent Groups
- Reread **Phonics Library** selections
- Finish *Practice Book, 102,* Blackline Master 36.
- Centers

Setting up the Centers

You will want to gather additional sets of three-step sequence cards prior to the Math Center activity on Day 2.

Phonics Center

Materials • Phonics Center materials for Theme 3, Week 3

Pairs work together to sort Picture Cards by beginning sound using the letters *t, s,* and *m*. See pages T125, T133, and T151 for this week's Phonics Center activities.

Writing Center

Materials • Blackline Master 55

Children draw and label a picture of something they like to do. See page T127 for this week's Writing Center activity.

Art Center

Materials • colored tissue paper • pipe cleaners

Children make colored tissue paper flowery in the Art Center. See page T131 for this week's Art Center activity.

 Dramatic Play Center

Children act out the folktale *The Amazing Little Porridge Pot.* See page T121 for this week's Dramatic Play Center.

 Math Center

Materials • Blackline Master 56–57

Children order sets of three-step sequence cards. Then they tell about the sequence of events using the order words *first, next,* and *last.* See page T137 for this week's Math Center activity.

Science Center

Materials • nonfiction picture books about the seasons • crayons and markers • drawing paper

Children look through picture books for ideas and then draw pictures of summer and winter activities. See page T141 for this week's Science Center activity.

Learning to Read
Day 1

Day at a Glance

Learning to Read

Read Aloud:

The Amazing Little Porridge Pot

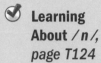 **Learning About / n /,** *page T124*

Word Work

✓ **High-Frequency Word Practice,** *page T126*

Writing & Language

Oral Language, *page T127*

☀ Half-Day Kindergarten

 Indicates lessons for tested skills. Choose additional activities as time allows.

Opening

Calendar

Sunday	Monday	Tuesday	Wednesday	Thursday	Friday	Saturday
			1	2	3	4
5	6	7	8	9	10	11
12	13	14	15	16	17	18
19	20	21	22	23	24	25
26	27	28	29	30	31	

Invite children to share what they did with their families over the weekend. Ask if they have any special family plans for the upcoming week.

Daily Message

Modeled Writing Model how to write the sounds you hear and talk about punctuation.

This week, we will hear a new story and reread some favorite family stories.

Have children chant the spelling of each word on the wall today: l-i-k-e *spells* like, m-y *spells* my, *capital* I *spells* I, s-e-e *spells* see.

Daily Phonemic Awareness
Beginning Sounds

- Tell children that they will play a listening game. *I will say three words. Two of the words will begin with the same sound. Listen carefully for words that begin with the same sound:* **pan, pull, dish.** *Yes,* **pan** *and* **pull** *begin with the same sound* /p/.

- Say the following three words, emphasizing the beginning sound in each: **nose, head, neck.** If necessary, repeat the words. When most hands are up, call on volunteers to identify the two words that begin with the same sound. *(nose, neck)* Continue with these words: *soap, seven, fan; jam, jet, bug; came, hat, hand; cup, pizza, pen; man, moon, run; ten, lock, tall; funny, see, fish.*

Getting Ready to Learn

To help plan their day, tell children that they will

- listen to a story called *The Amazing Little Porridge Pot.*

- meet a new Alphafriend, Nyle Noodle.

- act out a story in the Dramatic Play Center.

Read Aloud

Purposes • oral language • listening strategy • comprehension skill

Selection Summary
To repay her kindness, a man gives a woman a magical pot that cooks porridge on demand. All goes awry, however, when the woman's daughter uses the pot in her mother's absence and doesn't remember how to stop it.

Key Concept
Following directions

English Language Learners

Use the story art to help introduce story vocabulary such as: *cottage, woods, pot, porridge, daughter,* and *villages.* Encourage children to repeat the words "Cook, little pot, cook." And "Stop, little pot, stop." when your read this part.

Teacher Read Aloud
Oral Language/Comprehension

▶ Building Background

Tell children that the next story they will hear is a story called *The Amazing Little Porridge Pot*. Recall with children what porridge is from *Goldilocks and the Three Bears*, and have them speculate how a *porridge pot* might be used.

Strategy: Summarize

Teacher Modeling Tell children that good readers think about the important parts of a story so that they can retell it in their own words. Model how to summarize as you display the selection illustration.

> **Think Aloud**
>
> *When I look at this picture, I see a girl and a pot with porridge pouring out of it. As I read, I will listen for information that tells me more about the girl and the pot. This will help me to retell the story in my own words.*

✓ Comprehension Focus:
Inferences: Drawing Conclusions

Teacher Modeling Model how to use story and picture clues along with what you already know to decide how a story might turn out.

> **Think Aloud**
>
> *I know that sometimes a pot can bubble over. But I've never seen one boil over this much! Maybe this is a make-believe story. I'll use what I know to decide more about this story. You can do it too.*

▶ Listening to the Story

Read the story aloud, emphasizing the kindness of the woman and the impatience and frustration of the daughter. Pause at the discussion points to allow children to evaluate the story characters and draw conclusions. Note that Read Aloud art is also available on the back of the Theme Poster.

▶ Responding

Summarizing the Story Help children summarize parts of the story.

- *Who gave the porridge pot to the woman?*

- *What special instructions did the little man give the woman?*

- *Why did the daughter have trouble using the porridge pot?*

- *What happened when the pot wouldn't stop making porridge?*

- *How did the woman finally get the pot to stop?*

- *What lesson did the daughter learn?*

Practice Book pages 93–94 Children will complete the pages at small group time.

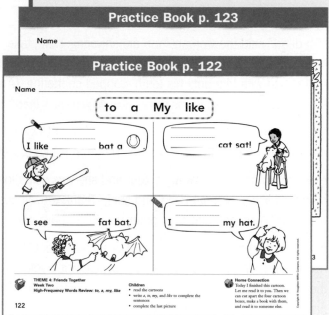

At Group Time

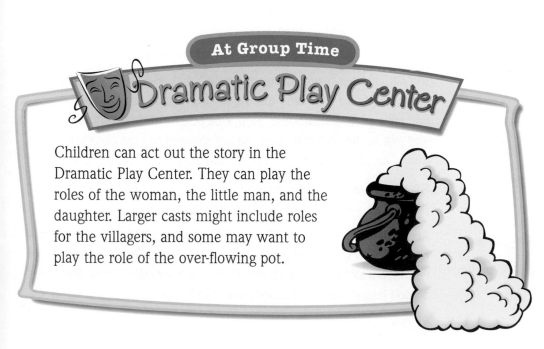

Dramatic Play Center

Children can act out the story in the Dramatic Play Center. They can play the roles of the woman, the little man, and the daughter. Larger casts might include roles for the villagers, and some may want to play the role of the over-flowing pot.

Teacher's Note

Some children may recognize the plot of this story as being similar to that of *Strega Nona* by Tomie de Paola. In this story Strega Nona's impatient apprentice tries to use a spaghetti pot. You may wish to read *Strega Nona* to children and have them compare and contrast the two tales.

Day 1

The Amazing Little Porridge Pot

A Danish Folktale

Long, long ago, a very kind woman and her daughter lived in a cottage in the woods. Because they had no well, the woman had to walk over a mile each day to a stream to get water for their morning porridge. Some mornings, the weather was very cold, and some mornings it was very hot, but every morning, the woman was very tired when she got back home with the water.

One very cold and snowy day, as the woman was making her way back from the stream, she was surprised to see a tiny little man, dressed in a light-weight coat and shivering in the wind.

"Oh dear!" said the woman. "You are shivering. Here, take my scarf to keep you warm." And she wrapped her warm scarf around the little man and stayed with him until his teeth stopped chattering. **(Ask:** *What do you know about the woman in this story? How do you know that?***)**

"You are so very kind," said the little man. "I want to give you something in return." And he pulled a small iron pot from his knapsack.

Now the woman was growing colder and she was still a long way from home, so she shook her head and said, "Thank you, sir. You, too, are kind. But I have no need of another pot. See, I have one in my hand."

But the little man insisted. "This is a very special pot," he said. "Take it home, put it on the fire, and say, 'Cook, little pot, cook!' and it will cook the most delicious porridge for you and your daughter. Then, when you have had enough, just say, 'Stop, little pot, stop!' And it will stop all by itself. But mind what I say. You *must* remember to use just these words and no others! Or you'll be sorry!" **(Ask:** *What do you suppose might happen if the woman doesn't follow the directions exactly? Let's find out.***)**

The woman didn't really believe the little man but, not wishing to be rude, she thanked him, and headed home with a pot in each hand. When she got there, she placed the pot on the stove and said, "Cook, little pot, cook!" And just as the little man had told her, something in the pot began to boil and bubble and the smell of a porridge filled the room. The woman was delighted at her good fortune. She called her daughter in to eat and together they ate until they could eat no more. They agreed that it was the most delicious porridge they had ever eaten.

The very next day, the woman rose early to go and find the little man so she could thank him for the amazing little porridge pot. She left the cottage before it was light, and long before her daughter got up.

When the daughter did get up, she was very hungry and couldn't wait for her mother to return. (You see, she was often just a little impatient.) Instead, she decided to make the porridge all by herself.

The girl put the pot on the stove and said, "Now what? Oh yes, I remember the words. 'Cook, little pot, cook!'" Sure enough, delicious smelling porridge started to boil and bubble. The girl scooped up a bowl and ate breakfast without waiting for her mother. **(Ask:** *Do you think it was a good idea for the girl to use the pot without her mother? Why?***)**

When next she looked, the porridge was still bubbling and beginning to spill over the sides of the pot. "Stop now! I've had enough!" the girl said. But the pot didn't stop. The porridge spilled onto the floor. The girl tried scooping it into a bigger pot, but it kept bubbling out.

"Enough!" she cried. "I am finished. Don't you hear me?" And she began to cry and stomp her feet and yell at the little pot. But the porridge just kept on boiling and bubbling out of the little pot. **(Ask:** *What's going on here? Why doesn't the pot stop?***)**

Out the cottage door flowed the porridge, down the path, and into the street. There was more porridge than anyone had ever seen! When the neighbors saw and smelled it, they grabbed their bowls and pots and scooped up as much as they could. But the porridge just kept flowing.

The girl's mother heard all the commotion and noise from where she was in the woods, so she came running home. As soon as she realized what had happened, she shouted "Stop, little pot, stop!" in a very, loud voice. And just as the little man said, the pot stopped making porridge. But what a mess there was to clean up. And guess who had to do most of it.

From that day on, the woman and her daughter—and all the villagers for that matter—never needed to make porridge again.

And it was then that the girl learned an important lesson that made her change her ways. She began to listen carefully, to follow directions exactly, and to wait for her mother before she tried something new. And that's a good lesson for all of us, don't you think?

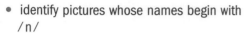
OBJECTIVES

Children

- identify pictures whose names begin with /n/

MATERIALS

- **Alphafriend Cards** *Benny Bear, Nyle Noodle, Tiggy Tiger*
- **Alphafriend Audiotape 00**
- **Alphafolder 00**
- **Picture Cards** *ball, berries, nine, nose, nurse, tooth, toys*
- **Phonics Center:** Theme 3, Week 3, Day 1

Home Connection

A take-home version of Nyle Noodle's song is an **Alphafriend Blackline Master.** Children can share the song with their families.

English Language Learners

English language learners will likely know what noodles are but may not know the word in English. If possible, bring in several types of *noodles* for children to examine. Say that all of these are noodles. Have children practice saying the word. Introduce *Nyle Noodle.* Ask children for other words they know that begin with the /n/ sound.

Phonemic Awareness
✔️ Beginning Sound

▶ Introducing the Alphafriend: Nyle Noodle

Tell children that today they will meet a new Alphafriend. Have children listen as you share a riddle to help them guess who their new Alphafriend is.

1 **Alphafriend Riddle** Read these clues:

- *Our Alphafriend's sound is /n/. Say it with me: /n/.*

- *This Alphafriend is a nnnarrow, flat, strip of dough.*

- *When he is cooked, he tastes nnnice with butter or sauce.*

- *His nnnname is also a nnnickname for a silly person.*

When most hands are up, call on children until they guess *noodle.*

2 **Pocket Chart** Display Nyle Noodle in a pocket chart. Say his name, stretching the /n/ sound slightly, and have children echo this.

3 📼 **Alphafriend Audiotape** Play Nyle Noodle's song. Listen for /n/ words in Nyle's song.

4 **Alphafolder** Have children find the /n/ pictures in the scene.

5 **Summarize**

- *What is our Alphafriend's name? What is his sound?*

- *What words in our Alphafriend's song start with /n/?*

- *Each time you look at Nyle this week, remember the /n/ sound.*

Nyle Noodle's Song
(Tune: "Farmer in the Dell")

I see a noodle named Nyle.
He likes to nap for a while.
He wears a scarf around
   his neck.
He's neat and very in style!

▶ Listening for / n /

Compare and Review: / b /, / t / Display Alphafriends *Benny Bear* and *Tiggy Tiger* opposite *Nyle Noodle*. Review each character's sound.

Tell children you'll name some pictures, and they should signal "thumbs up" for pictures that start with Nyle Noodle's sound, / n /. Volunteers put the card below Nyle's pictures. For "thumbs down" words, volunteers put cards below the correct Alphafriends.

Pictures: *nose, ball, tooth, nine, berries, toys, nurse*

Tell children that they will sort more pictures in the Phonics Center today.

▶ Apply

Practice Book pages 95–96 Children will complete the pages at small group time.

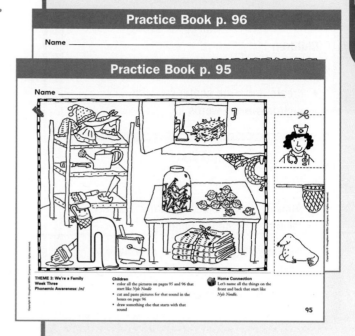

Practice Book p. 96

Name _____

Practice Book p. 95

Name _____

At Group Time

Phonics Center

Use the Phonics Center materials for **Theme 3, Week 3, Day 1**.

High-Frequency Word Practice

▶ Matching Words

■ Display Word Cards for the high-frequency words *I, like, my*, and *see* in a pocket chart. Call on children to identify each word and to match it on the Word Wall.

■ Remind children that these words are often found in books. *I'll read a poem. You listen to hear if these words are used in it.*

■ Read the poem "Everybody Says" on page 6 of *Higglety Pigglety. Did you hear any of these words in the poem?*
Let's see which Word Cards you can match to the words in the poem. (*I, like, my*)

THEME 7

Everybody Says

Everybody says
I look just like my mother.
Everybody says
I'm the image of Aunt Bee.
Everybody says
My nose is like my father's.
But I want to look like ME!

by Dorothy Aldis

6

Higglety Pigglety: A Book of Rhymes, page 6

Writing Opportunity Place the Word Cards *I like my* in a pocket chart. Have children read the words with you. Then display assorted Picture Cards and ask children to complete the sentence. Children can write and illustrate one of the sentences or use the words to create their own sentences with rebus pictures.

OBJECTIVES

Children
• read high-frequency words
• create and write sentences with high-frequency words

MATERIALS

• **Word Cards** *I, like, my, see*
• **Picture Cards** *blue, boat, toys*; choose others for sentence building
• *Higglety Pigglety: A Book of Rhymes,* page 6
• **Punctuation Card:** period

Oral Language

▶ Using Action Words

Tell children that some words are verbs, or action words. These words tell what a person or a thing does. Display *Tortillas and Lullabies* and help children recall the selection. Look at the pictures with the children and ask them to name some action words.

- Display pages 4 and 5, and have children tell what is happening. (great-grandmother and grandmother cooking tortillas)

- Write *cook tortillas* on chart paper. *Which word tells what a person does? That's right,* cook. Cook *is an action word.* Underline *cook.*

- Page through the book and ask children to tell what the people are doing. Help children identify the appropriate action word as needed.

cook tortillas

mix dough

grind corn

fry dough

press dough

OBJECTIVES

Children
- use action words

MATERIALS

- **Big Book:** *Tortillas and Lullabies*

At Group Time

Writing Center

Materials • Blackline Master 55

Put the chart in the Writing Center, so that children can read it on their own or with a friend. Children can complete **Blackline Master 55** by drawing a picture of something they like to do. Some children will be able to label their pictures with an action word.

I like to ride.

MEETING INDIVIDUAL NEEDS — English Language Learners

Introduce the concept of action words with verbs English language learners are likely to know. Call out a common verb, such as *jump, sing, dance, swim, cry.* Invite the class to perform the action. English language learners who do not yet know the word can follow their classmates example.

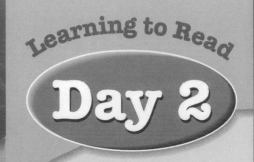

Day 2

Day at a Glance

Learning to Read

Big Book:

Tortillas and Lullabies

✓ **Phonics: Initial Consonant n,** *page T132*

✓ **High-Frequency Word Review:** *my, like, page T134*

Word Work

High-Frequency Word Practice, *page T136*

Writing & Language

Vocabulary Expansion, *page T137*

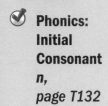

Half-Day Kindergarten

✓ Indicates lessons for tested skills. Choose additional activities as time allows.

Calendar

Sunday	Monday	Tuesday	Wednesday	Thursday	Friday	Saturday
			1	2	3	4
5	6	7	8	9	10	11
12	13	14	15	16	17	18
19	20	21	22	23	24	25
26	27	28	29	30	31	

Incorporate action words into the calendar routine. *It's sunny today. What things can you do outside on a sunny day? on a rainy day?* (play ball, run, skip; jump in puddles)

Daily Message

Modeled Writing After writing the daily message, allow children to come up and identify a letter or a word that they recognize. Give each child a chance to circle something. When children see how many items have been circled, they will be impressed with how much they have learned.

Today, we will bake many cookies. Sarah and Serena brought in 2 toads.

Distribute Word Cards for the words on the Word Wall. Have children match the cards to those on the Word Wall. After a match is made, have other children chant the spelling of the word: **m-y** *spells* my; **l-i-k-e** *spells* like.

....

 ## Daily Phonemic Awareness
Beginning Sounds

- Read "Oodles of Noodles" on page 17 of *Higglety Pigglety.*

- Tell children that they will play What's the Sound? *I will say a word from the poem. You listen for the beginning sound and tell me the sound your hear. Now listen:* nnnoodles.

- When most hands are up, have children voice the sound. *Yes, /n/ is the sound at the beginning of* noodles.

- Continue in a similar manner with other words from the poem: *love, mound, sun, favorite, foodles, ton.*

Higglety Pigglety: A Book of Rhymes, page 17

Getting Ready to Learn

To help plan their day, tell children that they will

- reread and talk about the Big Book: *Tortillas and Lullabies.*

- learn the new letters, *N* and *n,* and see pictures that begin with *n.*

- make paper flowers in the Art Center.

Day 2
Learning to Read

Big Book

HOUGHTON MIFFLIN
Reading

Tortillas and Lullabies
Tortillas y cancioncitas

BY **LYNN REISER**
PICTURES BY "CORAZONES VALIENTES"

Includes:
Social Studies Link

Purposes • concepts of print • story language
• reading strategy • comprehension skill

Sharing the Big Book
Oral Language/Comprehension

▶ Building Background

Reading for Understanding *You remember this book, Tortillas and Lullabies. As we read the story this time, look for clues in the pictures that tell you more about the setting and what the characters are doing.*

Strategy: Summarize

Student Modeling Remind children that good readers think about the important parts of a story so that they can retell the story later. *This story is organized in a special way that helps us to remember the different parts. What are the four parts in the story?*

Comprehension Focus:
Story Structure: Characters/Setting

Student Modeling *Who is the telling the story? What characters are in the story? Where does the story take place?*

▶ Sharing the Story

Reread the story, pausing for these discussion points:

pages 4–7
Story Structure: Setting

■ *Last time, we noticed the setting was at a home, but I also see something else. Do you see something that shows the place is the same?* (the volcano)

pages 12–17
Noting Details

■ *How do these pictures show how the land has changed?* (The animals have gone from wild forest animals to farm animals to pets.)

pages 20–23

Compare and Contrast

■ *How are the ways the girl's great-grandmother, grandmother, and mother washed clothes alike? How are they different?*

pages 28–32

Evaluate

■ *Why was the lullaby the same every time?* (It was a family tradition.)

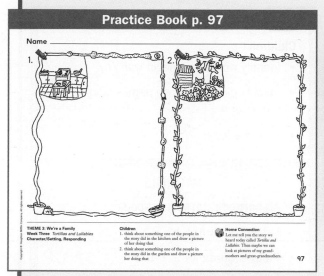

▶ **Responding**

Story Talk Page through the book, asking children to use the pictures to tell how the actions of the different generations of the family are alike and different.

Practice Book page 97 Children will complete this page at small group time.

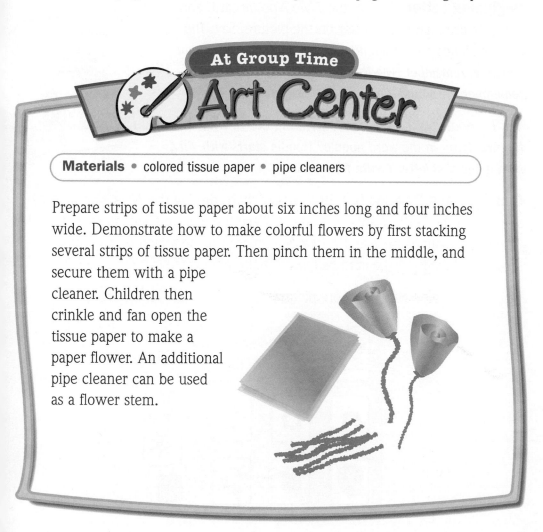

At Group Time

Art Center

Materials • colored tissue paper • pipe cleaners

Prepare strips of tissue paper about six inches long and four inches wide. Demonstrate how to make colorful flowers by first stacking several strips of tissue paper. Then pinch them in the middle, and secure them with a pipe cleaner. Children then crinkle and fan open the tissue paper to make a paper flower. An additional pipe cleaner can be used as a flower stem.

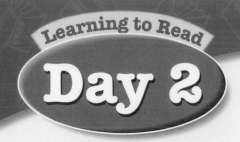

Learning to Read
Day 2

OBJECTIVES

Children

- identify words that begin with /n/
- identify pictures whose names start with the letter *n*
- form the letters *Nn*

MATERIALS

- **Alphafriend Card** *Nyle Noodle*
- **Letter Cards** *n, t, b*
- **Picture Cards** for *n, t, b*
- **Blackline Master 170**
- **Phonics Center:** Theme 3, Week 3, Day 2

Extra Support

To help children remember the sound for *n*, point out that the letter's *name* gives a clue to its sound: *n*, /n/.

Phonics

✓ *Initial Consonant* n

....

▶ Develop Phonemic Awareness

Beginning Sound Read the lyrics to Nyle Noodle's song and have children echo it line-for-line. Have them listen for /n/ words and "nod" each time they hear one.

> **Nyle Noodle's Song**
> (Tune: "Farmer in the Dell")
>
> I see a noodle named Nyle.
> He likes to nap for a while.
> He wears a scarf around
>   his neck.
> He's neat and very in style!

....

▶ Connect Sounds to Letters

Beginning Letter Display the *Nyle Noodle* card, and have children name the letter on the picture. Say: *The letter* n *stands for the sound /n/, as in* noodle. *When you see an* n, *remember* Nyle Noodle. *That will help you remember the sound /n/.*

Write *noodle* on the board, underlining the *n*. *What is the first letter in the word* noodle? Noodle *starts with /n/, so* n *is the first letter I write for* noodle.

Compare and Review: *b, t* In a pocket chart, display the *Nyle Noodle* card along with the Letter Cards *n, b,* and *t*. Place the Picture Cards in random order. Review the sounds for *b* and *t*. In turn, children name a picture, say the beginning sound, and put the card below the right letter.

Tell children they will sort more pictures in the Phonics Center today.

▶ Handwriting

Writing *N, n* Tell children that now they'll learn to write the letters that stand for /n/: capital *N* and small *n*. Write each letter as you recite the handwriting rhyme. Children can chant each rhyme as they "write" the letter in the air

Handwriting Rhyme: N

A line that goes down.
Then a slide
to the side.
One more line down.
Big *N*, we cried!

Handwriting Rhyme: n

Little *n* is short.
One line down
at the start.
Then one little hill.
That's the fun part.

▶ Apply

Practice Book page 98 Children will complete this page at small group time.

Blackline Master 170 This page provides additional handwriting practice.

At Group Time

Phonics Center

Use the Phonics Center materials for **Theme 3, Week 3, Day 2**.

Teacher's Note

Handwriting practice for the continuous stroke style is available on **Blackline Master 196**.

Portfolio Opportunity

Save the Practice Book page to show children's grasp of the letter-sound association.
Save **Blackline Master 170** for a handwriting sample.

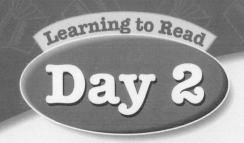
✓ High-Frequency Words

Review Words: my, like

▶ Teach

Tell children that today they will practice reading and writing two words that they will see often in stories. Say *my* and call on volunteers to use the word in a sentence. Write *my* on the board, and have children spell it as you point to the letters. Spell *my* with me, *m-y, my.* Then lead children in a chant, clapping on each beat, to help them remember the spelling: *m-y, my! m-y, my.*

Repeat for the word *like.*

Word Wall Have children find the words *my* and *like* on the Word Wall. Remind children to look there when they need to remember how to write the words.

▶ Practice

Reading Build the following sentences in a pocket chart. Children can take turns reading the sentences aloud. Place the pocket chart in the Phonics Center along with additional Picture Cards so that children can practice building and reading sentences.

Display *Higglety Pigglety: A Book of Rhymes*, page 6.

- Share the poem "Everybody Says" aloud.

- Reread the poem. *I'll read the poem one more time. This time, listen for the word* my. *If you hear it raise your hand.* Children should raise their hands three times.

- Call on children to point to the word *my* each time it appears in the poem.

- Repeat for the word *like*, which also appears three times.

THEME 1

Everybody Says

Everybody says
I look just like my mother.
Everybody says
I'm the image of Aunt Bee.
Everybody says
My nose is like my father's.
But I want to look like ME!

by Dorothy Aldis

6

***Higglety Pigglety: A Book of Rhymes*, page 6**

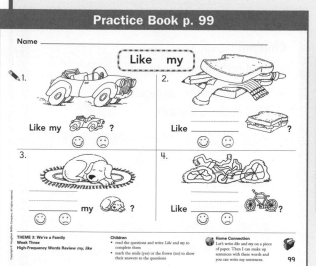

Practice Book p. 99

▶ Apply

Practice Book page 99 Children will read and write *my* and *like* as they complete the Practice Book page.

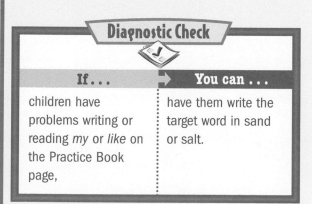

Diagnostic Check

If...	You can...
children have problems writing or reading *my* or *like* on the Practice Book page,	have them write the target word in sand or salt.

High-Frequency Word (T135)

OBJECTIVES

Children

- read high-frequency words
- create and write sentences with high-frequency words

MATERIALS

- **Word Cards** *I, like, my, see*
- **Picture Cards** *dog, watch;* choose others for sentence building
- **Punctuation Card:** period, question mark

High-Frequency Word Practice

▶ Building Sentences

Tell children that you need their help to build a question.

■ Display the Word Cards and Picture Cards in random order. Tell children that you will use these words to build your question. Review the words together. Then explain that you are ready to build the sentence.

■ *I want the first word to be* See. *Who can find that word? Good, I want the next word to be* my. *Which card should I use? Who can read the sentence so far?*

■ Place Picture Card *watch* and a question mark at the end to complete the sentence *See my [watch]?*

■ Read the completed sentence together, then continue with a new one: *I like my [watch].*

Writing Opportunity Have children copy a sentence from the pocket chart and illustrate it. Some children may wish to complete the sentence stems using their own rebus suggestions.

Vocabulary Expansion

▶ Using Order Words

Recall that yesterday children listed action words from the book *Tortillas and Lullabies.* Display the chart and review it with children. (See page T127).

Viewing and Speaking Tell children that now they will use the clues in the picture to figure out the steps needed to make tortillas.

■ Revisit the pictures on pages 4 to 7 of *Tortillas and Lullabies.* Prompt children to help them order the steps in making tortillas: ***What did great-grandmother do first, grind the corn into flour or mix the dough? What did she do next, press the dough into a round circle or fry it?***

■ Write numerals by the items on yesterday's chart to order the steps. Then write the directions on chart paper. Read the completed directions, emphasizing the order words.

> ### How to Cook Tortillas
> First, grind the corn.
> Next, mix the dough.
> Then, press the dough.
> Last, fry the dough.

At Group Time
Math Center

Materials • Blackline Masters 56–57 or sequence cards

Duplicate **Blackline Masters 56–57** or prepare three-step sequence cards and place them in the Math Center. Have children put the cards in the correct order and use the order words *first, next,* and *last* to tell about the sequence.

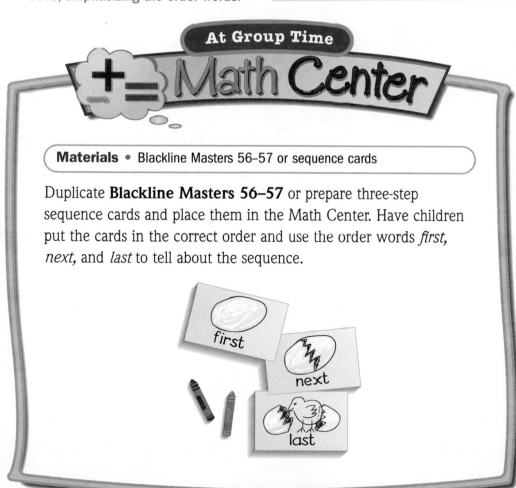

English Language Learners

Children may not be familiar with order words. Teach those words gradually. Use concrete situations, such as children in line to ask questions using order words. For example: "Who is *first* in line today?"

Day at a Glance

Learning to Read

Big Book:

Shoes From Grandpa

☑ **Phonics:**
Initial
Consonant *n*,
page T142

Word Work

Exploring Words, *page T144*

Writing & Language

Shared Writing, *page T145*

 Half-Day Kindergarten

☑ Indicates lessons for tested skills. Choose additional activities as time allows.

Opening

Calendar

Sunday	Monday	Tuesday	Wednesday	Thursday	Friday	Saturday
			1	2	3	4
5	6	7	8	9	10	11
12	13	14	15	16	17	18
19	20	21	22	23	24	25
26	27	28	29	30	31	

After conducting the calendar routine, review the days of the week. Ask children to share special plans for the week.

Daily Message

Modeled Writing Incorporate class events into the daily message. Where appropriate, encourage children to share the pen.

Today we have library after snack.

Ask children to find the two new words that they added to the Word Wall this theme. Have them chant the spelling of each word: **l-i-k-e** *spells* like; **m-y** *spells* my. Continue in a similar manner with the remaining words.

Routines

 Daily Phonemic Awareness
Beginning Sounds

- *Let's play Name That Word. You will listen for beginning sounds. I will say two words, you tell me which word begins with Nyle Noodle's sound, /n/. Listen:* nnnext, lllast.

- *Say the words with me:* nnnext, lllast. *Which word begins with /n/?... Yes,* next *begins with /n/.*

- Continue with the words shown.

no/quiet	sing/none
new/doctor	ball/nurse
noisy/yes	ten/narrow
dog/night	north/side

Getting Ready to Learn

To help plan their day, tell children that they will

- reread and talk about the Big Book *Shoes From Grandpa.*

- read a story called "Cat's Surprise."

- explore summer and winter activities in the Science Center.

Big Book

HOUGHTON MIFFLIN
Reading

SHOES FROM GRANDPA
by MEM FOX • Illustrated by PATRICIA MULLINS

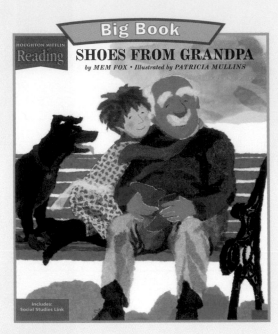

Includes:
Social Studies Link

Purposes • concepts of print • story language
• reading strategy • comprehension skill

Extra Support

Review the story pictures with children, having them point to and name various articles of clothing.

Sharing the Big Book
Oral Language/Comprehension

▶ **Building Background**

Reading for Understanding *You remember* Shoes From Grandpa. *This time when we read it, let's see if you can use the picture clues to name each family member and what that person wants to get Jessie.*

Strategy: Summarize

Student Modeling *As we read, what story parts will you think about to help you remember the story so that you can retell it?* (setting; characters)

✓ Comprehension Focus:
Inferences: Drawing Conclusions

Student Modeling *Which present is Jessie the most excited about? Why? Do you think Jessie is happy with all of her presents? Why or why not?*

▶ **Sharing the Story**

Reread the story, pausing for these discussion points:

✓ **pages 10–11**
Drawing Conclusions

■ *Why do you think Jessie's mom says she'll buy a skirt that won't show the dirt? Why won't this skirt show the dirt?*

pages 12–13
Evaluate

■ *Jessie's cousin says she'll look for a blouse with ribbons and bows. Is this a blouse that Jessie would like or one her cousin would like? Why?*

pages 23–24

Categorize and Classify

■ *What hats do you see? Shoes? Can you find three disguises?*

 pages 28–29

Drawing Conclusions

■ *Why do you think Jessie wants jeans?*

....

▶ **Responding**

Retelling Children take turns retelling the story using picture clues as prompts. If necessary, allow children to go through the book more than once so all children have a chance to participate.

At Group Time

Science Center

> **Materials** • nonfiction picture books about the seasons • drawing paper • crayons or markers

Place nonfiction picture books about the seasons in the Science Center. Have children browse through the books. Then ask them to draw pictures to show summer activities and winter activities. Allow time for children share their pictures and compare the activities with those of their classmates.

Learning to Read

Day 3

✓ Initial Consonant n

Practice Book p. 100

Name _____

THEME 3: We're a Family
Week Three
Phonics: Initial Consonant *n*

100

Children
• for 1 and 2, write *Nn* beside the pictures whose names start like *Nyle Noodle*
• for 3, draw two things that start with the sound for *n*

Home Connection
Let me tell you about the things on the page that begin with the sound for *n*.

Extra Support

Read "Oodles of Noodles," on *Higglety Pigglety: A Book of Rhymes*, page 17. Have children "nod" their heads each time them hear a word that begins with / n /. Then call on volunteers to point to words that begin with *n* in the rhyme.

▶ Develop Phonemic Awareness

Beginning Sound Read the lyrics to Nyle Noodle's song aloud, and have children tap their desks when they hear / n / words.

Tell children that you will read the song again. *This time, if you hear a word that begins with / n / stand up. If you hear another / n / word, sit back down. We'll do this each time we hear an / n / word.* As needed, model standing and sitting alternately for / n / words as you read the first line. Then say the entire song, having just children stand and sit for / n / words.

> ### Nyle Noodle's Song
> (Tune: "Farmer in the Dell")
>
> I see a noodle named Nyle.
> He likes to nap for a while.
> He wears a scarf around
>   his neck.
> He's neat and very in style!

▶ Connect Sounds to Letters

Beginning Letter *n* Display the *Nyle Noodle* card and have children name the letter on the picture. *What letter stands for the sound / n /, as in* noodle? (*n*) *Who can help you remember the sound / n /?* (Nyle Noodle)

Write *noodle* on the board, underlining the *n*. *What is the first letter in the word* noodle? (*n*) *Noodle starts with / n /, so* n *is the first letter I write for* noodle.

Compare and Review: *b, t* Display the Letter Cards for *n, b,* and *t* on the chalkboard ledge. Review the sounds for *b* and *t* with children. Then distribute Picture Cards for *n, b,* and *t,* one to a child, to a group of children. In turn, children name their picture, say the beginning sound, and stand by the correct letter on the board ledge.

Repeat the activity with different groups of children until each child has a chance to name a picture, say the beginning sound, and stand beside the correct letter.

▶ Apply

Practice Book page 100 Children complete the page at small group time.

Phonics in Action

Phonics Library

We're a Family

Applying Skills

Purposes
- read a wordless story
- find pictures beginning with /n/

Cat's Surprise
by Susan Gorman-Howe
illustrated by Valeri Gorbachev

17

▶ Introducing the Story

Let's read the title. It says Cat's Surprise. *The picture on the title page shows a family and a cat. Do you think the surprise is* for *the cat or* from *the cat?*

Discuss the picture on the title page. Point out that the picture is a portrait of the family.

Let's look at the pictures to see what the story is about. Do a picture walk and guide children in a discussion of the pictures.

18   19

▶ Coached Reading

Have children carefully look at each page before discussing it with you. Prompts:

page 18   *Who is the dish of food for?*

page 19   *What are the boy and his sister doing?*

page 21   *Why do you think that everyone looks happy? What you do think they found?*

pages 22-23   *What do you see on these pages? What is the cat's surprise?*

Now let's go back and look at each page to find things that begin with Nyle Noodle's sound, /n/.

20   21

22   23

Home Connection

Children can color the pictures in the take-home version of "Cat's Surprise." After rereading on Day 4, they can take it home to read to family members.

Phonics   **T143**

DAY 3

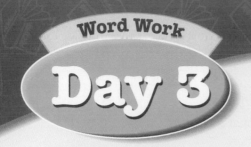

MATERIALS

• **Big Book:** *Shoes From Grandpa*

• *From Apples to Zebras: A Book of ABC's*

Exploring Words

▶ Environmental Print

Display pages 24 and 25 of *Shoes From Grandpa*. Have children recall what Jessie's uncle said that he would buy. **Yes, mittens! Now look at the picture. Can you tell what else this store sells? How do you know?** (socks, hats; The signs show what is for sale.)

■ Begin a discussion of environmental print. Explain that there are many signs around the school and in their neighborhood that help people, just as the signs in the store did.

■ Brainstorm with children signs that they have seen in their neighborhood and around the school. Prompt children as needed: **What signs do you see on the bathroom doors at school? What signs do you see at street corners?** (*Stop* sign, *Walk/Don't Walk* signs) **What sign do we see near the doors at school?** (*exit* signs; *push/pull*; *in/out*)

■ Begin a list on chart paper to record children's suggestions. As time permits, you may want to take a walk with the children around the school, both inside and outside, to look for other examples.

Writing Opportunity Have children draw pictures of signs they have seen around the school or in their neighborhood. Children can refer to the class chart or the examples in *From Apples to Zebras: A Book of ABC's.*

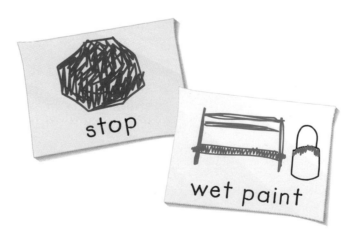

Shared Writing

▶ ## Using Order Words

Listening and Speaking Recall with children that yesterday they used order words to show the steps needed to make tortillas. Display the chart and review it with children.

■ Remind children that order words are important to following directions. Recall the problems the girl had in *The Amazing Little Porridge Pot* when she did not follow directions. Then ask children to listen carefully as you reread the little man's directions on how to use the pot (page T122, paragraph 6).

■ *What should the woman do first?* (Put the pot on the fire.) *What should she do next, to make the pot cook?* (Say, "Cook, little pot, cook!") *What should she do then?* (eat until she has had enough) *What should she do last, to make the pot stop?* (Say, "Stop, little pot, stop!")

Have children take turns using the words *first, next, then*, and *last* to give directions on how to use the little porridge pot.

■ After several volunteers have had a chance to retell the directions, write them on chart paper. Ask children to help you think of a good title for the directions.

How to Use the Little Pot

First, put the pot on the fire.
Next say, "Cook, little pot, cook!"
Then eat all the porridge you want.
Last say, "Stop, little pot, stop!"

DAY 3

 English Language Learners

To have children use order words, have a wordless story with the pictures out of order. Help them decide which picture comes first, second, etc. Emphasize the use of order words to describe the pictures.

Day 4

Day at a Glance

Learning to Read

Big Book:

Families

 Phonics:
Review Initial
Consonant *n*,
page T150

Word Work

Exploring Words, *page T152*

Writing & Language

Interactive Writing, *page T153*

Half-Day Kindergarten

 Indicates lessons for tested skills. Choose additional activities as time allows.

Opening

Calendar

Sunday	Monday	Tuesday	Wednesday	Thursday	Friday	Saturday
			1	2	3	4
5	6	7	8	9	10	11
12	13	14	15	16	17	18
19	20	21	22	23	24	25
26	27	28	29	30	31	

Remind children that Thursday night is Share a Book Night. Ask children what book they will share with their families tonight.

Daily Message

Modeled Writing Use some words that begin with *n* in today's message, as in the example shown. Call on volunteers to circle the *n*'s.

> The school nurse will test our eyes today.
> Nadia is out sick today.

Read the Word Wall together. Then play a rhyming game: *I am going to find a word on the wall that rhymes with bee. Bee rhymes with... see. Raise your hand when you find a word that rhymes with sky.* (*I, my*)

Routines

✓ Daily Phonemic Awareness
Beginning Sounds

- *Listen as I say two words:* nnnote, nnnice. *Say the words with me:* nnnote, nnnice. *Do you hear the same sound at the beginning of each word?... Yes,* note *and* nice *begin with the same sound.* Help children isolate the beginning sound, /n/.

- Play a listening game with children. Explain that you will say two words that begin with the same sound. They should raise their hands when they know the sound.

- Say the following pairs of words. For each pair, have children isolate and identify the beginning sound.

ribbon/rocket	tomato/tunnel
night/now	marble/magnet
sister/see	porridge/pond
button/basket	newspaper/number

Getting Ready to Learn

To help plan their day, tell children that they will

- reread the Social Studies Links: *Families* and *Which Would You Choose?*

- sort pictures that begin with *n, s,* and *r.*

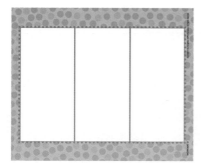

- reread a story called "Cat's Surprise."

Cat's Surprise
by Susan Gorman-Howe
illustrated by Valeri Gorbachev

OBJECTIVES

Children

- draw conclusions
- recognize use of capital letter at the beginning of a sentence
- recognize use of end punctuation: period, question mark
- observe use of directionality: return sweep

Big Book

pages 35–41

Before rereading, invite pairs of children to revisit the selections by taking picture walks through them. Children can take turns sharing what they remember about the selections, using the pictures as prompts.

Sharing the Big Books
Social Studies Links

▶ **Building Background**

Rereading for Understanding Display *Families* and children share what they remember about the selection. Reread the selection, pausing for discussion.

pages 36–37
Strategy: Evaluate

■ *How are these families like your family or other families you know? How are they different?*

 page 39
Comprehension Focus: Inferences: Drawing Conclusions

■ *This picture shows a couple and their children and grandchildren? Which two people are the grandparents? How do you know?*

 page 40
Concepts of Print: Capital at Beginning of Sentence, End Punctuation, Return Sweep

■ *What can you tell me about the beginning and end of this sentence? Who can show me with their hand how to read the words in this sentence?*

page 41
Noting Details

■ *What family members are in each picture? Where are the families?*

▶ **Responding**

Summarizing Have each child tell something they learned about families from this selection.

▶ Building Background

Rereading for Understanding Remind children that they also read *Which Would You Choose?* Pause for discussion as you share the selection.

title page
Strategy: Predict/Infer

■ *How does the cover help you predict what this selection is about?*

 page 34

Comprehension Focus: Inferences: Drawing Conclusions

■ *What clues tell you that Mom likes to garden?*

page 39
Evaluate

■ *How would you answer the questions on this page?*

▶ Responding

Literature Circle Have children tell how the selections *Families* and *Which Would You Choose?* are alike. Then have them tell how they are different.

At Group Time

Art Center

Materials • magazines • scissors

Have children cut out pictures of families playing together and working together. Make a class mural with the pictures.

OBJECTIVES

Children
• draw conclusions

Big Book

Social Studies Link

Which Would You Choose?

SHOES FROM GRANDPA
by MEM FOX • Illustrated by PATRICIA MULLINS

pages 33–39

DAY 4

MEETING INDIVIDUAL NEEDS **Challenge**

Some children will be able to develop *Which Would You Choose?* scenarios. Children can draw, or cut from magazines, pictures of different articles of clothing and pose questions to classmates; for example, "Jill needs a hat to ride her bike. Which would you choose?"

Sharing the Big Book **T149**

Day 4

Phonics

 Review Initial Consonant n

OBJECTIVES

Children

- identify words that begin with /n/
- identify pictures whose names start with the letter n

MATERIALS

- **Alphafriend Cards** *Nyle Noodle, Reggie Rooster, Sammy Seal*
- **Alphafolder** *Nyle Noodle*
- **Letter Cards** *n, r, s*
- **Picture Cards** for *n, r, s*
- ***From Apples to Zebras: A Book of ABC's,*** page 15
- **Phonics Center:** Theme 3, Week 3, Day 4

▶ **Develop Phonemic Awareness**

Beginning Sound Display the scene in Nyle Noodle's Alphafolder. *One thing I see is a napkin. Say* napkin *with me. Does* napkin *begin with the same sound as Nyle Noodle, /n/?* Call on volunteers to point to and name other items in the picture that begin with /n/.

▶ **Connect Sounds to Letters**

Review Consonant *n* Using self-stick notes, cover the words on page 15 of *From Apples to Zebras: A Book of ABC's.* Then display the page. Ask children what letter they expect to see first in each word and why. Uncover the words so that children can check their predictions.

Ask children to think of other words that begin with /n/. List their suggestions on the board. Have volunteers underline each *n.*

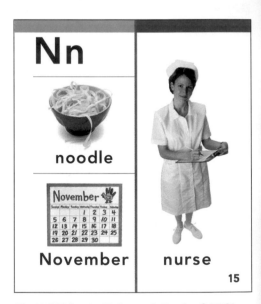

From Apples to Zebras: A Book of ABC's, page 15

newspaper   <u>n</u>ine
<u>n</u>apkins   <u>n</u>oisemaker
<u>n</u>eedles   (butterfly) <u>n</u>et
<u>n</u>umbers
<u>n</u>urse hat

Home Connection

Challenge children to look at home for items or for names that begin with the consonant *n.* Children can draw pictures to show what they have found.

▶ Apply

Compare and Review: r, s In a pocket chart, display the cards for *Nyle Noodle, Reggie Rooster*, and *Sammy Seal* and the Letter Cards *n, r*, and *s*. Review the sounds for *r*, /r/ and *s*, /s/.

Hold up Picture Cards one at a time. Have children signal "thumbs up" for pictures that begin with *n*, /n/. When all of Nyle's pictures are in place, repeat for *r*, /r/ and *s*, /s/.

Pictures: *bed, rope, six, boat, rake, red, sun, bike, sandals*

Tell children they will sort more pictures in the Phonics Center today.

Practice Book page 101 Children will complete this page at small group time.

Phonics Library In groups today, children will also identify pictures that begin with initial n as they reread the **Phonics Library** story "Cat's Surprise." See suggestions, page T143.

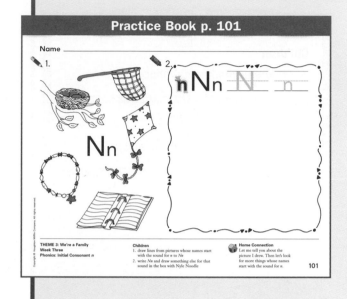

Practice Book p. 101

At Group Time

Phonics Center

Use the Phonics Center materials for **Theme 3, Week 3, Day 4**.

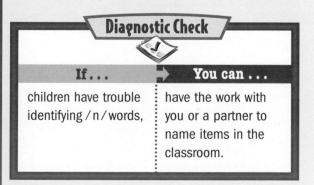

Diagnostic Check

If...	You can...
children have trouble identifying /n/ words,	have the work with you or a partner to name items in the classroom.

DAY 4

Phonics (T151)

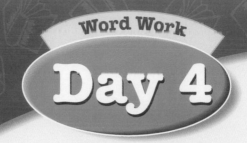
Exploring Words

▶ Environmental Print

Remind children that yesterday they talked about signs around the school and in the neighborhood that help people. Tell children that today they will talk about "signs" around our homes that help us.

■ Display page 8 of *Tortillas and Lullabies*. Ask if children can find something on the page that has words on it. Tell children that the bag says *masa rica* which means "rich flour." Then direct attention to page 17. Point out the glue bottle (*goma*). Lead children to see that these kinds of "signs" also help us.

■ Review the housekeeping corner of your classroom, examining items like cereal boxes, cans, and jars for signs or labels and "appliances" for words like *on* and *off*.

■ Discuss other signs and labels found in children's homes. ***Does your television have a button that says* power, channel, *or* volume? *What words might you see on a stove? on a washer or a dryer? Do you have a sign on your bedroom door?***

Writing Opportunity Tell children to look for signs when they go home. Ask children to draw a picture of one of the signs they see. Children can draw a picture of a product or an appliance with words on it. Some children may wish to make signs for their bedroom doors.

Interactive Writing

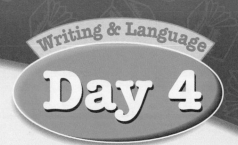

▶ ## Using Order Words

Speaking Recall with children that yesterday they used order words to write directions that told how to use the little porridge pot. Tell children that today they will write directions to tell how to do something that the class knows how to do.

■ Brainstorm with children possible topics for their directions. For example, children might suggest: how to fill the hamster's water bottle, how to access a class computer game, or what to do during a fire drill.

■ Help children choose a single topic. As needed, steer children to choose a topic that has a three- to four-step set of directions.

Once children have chosen the topic, write the words *first, next, then,* and *last* on chart paper. Have children take turns using the words to explain the order in which the steps should be followed to complete the task.

■ After several volunteers have a chance to retell the directions, write them on chart paper. Share the pen with children. They can write known beginning consonants and high-frequency words or add end punctuation.

■ Ask children to help you think of a good title for the directions.

OBJECTIVES

Children
• write directions using order words

 Portfolio Opportunity
Save children's writing as examples of their ability to write to task.

DAY 4

Learning to Read
Day 5

Day at a Glance

Learning to Read

Revisiting the Literature:

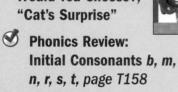

The Amazing Porridge Pot, Tortillas and Lullabies, Shoes From Grandpa, Families, Which One Would You Choose?, "Cat's Surprise"

☑ **Phonics Review: Initial Consonants *b, m, n, r, s, t*, page T158**

Word Work

Exploring Words, *page T160*

Writing & Language

Independent Writing, *page T161*

Half-Day Kindergarten

☑ Indicates lessons for tested skills. Choose additional activities as time allows.

Opening

Calendar

Sunday	Monday	Tuesday	Wednesday	Thursday	Friday	Saturday
			1	2	3	4
5	6	7	8	9	10	11
12	13	14	15	16	17	18
19	20	21	22	23	24	25
26	27	28	29	30	31	

Review with children any words that were added to the calendar this week. Call on volunteers to use the words in oral sentences.

Daily Message

Interactive Writing Share the pen with children. Have volunteers contribute letters or words that they can read and write.

It's time to look at all the books we have read. Which one did you like?

Distribute Word Cards for the words on the Word Wall. Have children match the cards to the words on the Word Wall. After a match is made, have other children chant the spelling of the word: **l-i-k-e** *spells* like.

Routines

Daily Phonemic Awareness
Beginning Sounds

- Play a guessing game with children.

- Secretly choose an action word, for example, *run.* Say: *I am thinking of something you do with your feet. This action word begins with /r/. What can you do with your feet that begins with /r/?*

- Allow children to guess, correcting them as needed or providing additional clues. *Yes, you do walk with your feet, but walk doesn't begin with /r/. I'm thinking of something you might do in a race.*

- Repeat several times with other action words until children have caught on to how to play. Then let children take turns thinking of action words.

Getting Ready to Learn

To help plan their day, tell children that they will

- talk about books they've read in We're a Family.

- take home a story they can read.

- write about families in their journals.

DAY 5

Technology

www.eduplace.com
Log on to **Education Place** for more activities relating to We're a Family.

www.bookadventure.org
This Internet reading-incentive program provides thousands of titles for children to read.

Revisiting the Literature

▶ Literature Discussion

Help children compare the different books you have shared this week: *The Amazing Little Porridge Pot, Tortillas and Lullabies, Shoes From Grandpa, Families, Which Would You Choose?* and "Cat's Surprise." Display the books one at a time. Use these suggestions to help children recall the selections.

- Ask what happened when the daughter tried to use the little porridge pot.

- Have children recall the four parts in *Tortillas and Lullabies.*

- Page through *Shoes From Grandpa*. Have children use the pictures as prompts to recall the things Jessie's family wanted to buy her.

- Take a picture walk of *Families*. Ask children what families do together.

- For *Which Would You Choose?* call on volunteers to tell how people choose the clothes they wear.

- Together, read "Cat's Surprise." Ask children to identify pictures in the story beginning with / n /.

- Children might also recall the Read Aloud selections *Jonathan and His Mommy* and *Goldilocks and the Three Bears*. Call on volunteers to tell what these stories were about.

- Have children vote for their favorite book, and then read the text of the winner aloud.

✓ **Comprehension Focus: Characters-Setting** Display the books, one at a time, and read the titles aloud. Have children recall the characters and settings in each one. Ask children to tell how the characters and settings were alike and different.

✓ **Comprehension Focus: Drawing Conclusions** Lead children in a discussion to tell how they used story and picture clues to make decisions about the characters and settings in the stories. After looking at each selection, help children develop a one- or two-sentence summary of it.

Nicky Takes a Bath

Leveled Books

On My Way Practice Reader

▶ Preparing to Read

Building Background Share the title, and explain that Nicky is a dog. Invite children who have pets to tell about them: *Do the animals like to be bathed? What happens at the pets' bath time?*

▶ Guiding the Storytelling

Look through the pictures and discuss them. Use the ideas below to prepare children for telling the story on their own.

page 1: *Who are the characters in the story? Let's give them names.*

pages 2–3: *What is Nicky doing? Do you think he likes bath time? What are the children doing?*

pages 4–5: *Does Nicky like his bubble bath? How are the children trying to make him feel better?*

pages 6–7: *What does Nicky do while they are washing his tail? What does he see outside? What might the children be saying?*

page 8: *Oh, my! What happened? Now what will the family have to do?*

Prompting the Storytellers As children take turns telling the story page by page, use prompts to reinforce their sense of story:

■ *What is the title of the story? Who is in it? Where does it take place?*

■ *How does the story begin? What happens next? And then what happens?*

■ *How does the story end? Would you have ended it the same way?*

▶ Responding

Phonics Connection Invite children to find pictures whose names start with /t/, /b/, or /n/. Then two children can retell the story while the others act it out. They might draw some dog toys and bones for "Nicky" to use as props.

The materials listed below provide reading practice for children at different levels.

Little Big Books

Little Readers for Guided Reading

Houghton Mifflin Classroom Bookshelf

DAY 5

Home Connection

Remind children to share the **take-home version** of "Cat's Surprise" with their families.

Revisiting the Literature/ Building Fluency

(T157)

Phonics Review

✓ Initial Consonants: b, m, n, r, s, t

OBJECTIVES ◎

Children

• review initial consonants *b, m, n, r, s, t*

• make sentences with high-frequency words

MATERIALS

• **Word Cards** *I, like, my, see*

• **Punctuation Card:** period

• **Picture Cards** for *b, m, n, r, s, t;* choose others for sentence building

---

▶ Review

Tell children that they will take turns naming pictures and telling what letter stands for the beginning sound.

■ Randomly place four Picture Cards, along the chalkboard ledge. Call on four children to come up and stand before a picture. In turn, have each child name the picture, isolate the initial sound, and write *b, m, n, r, s,* or *t* on the chalkboard above the picture.

■ Have the rest of the class verify that the correct letter has been written above each picture. Then write the picture name on the board and underline the initial consonant.

■ Continue with other pictures.

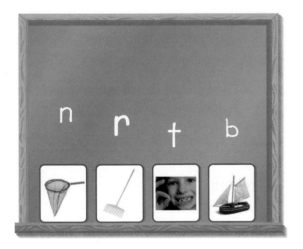

High-Frequency Word Review

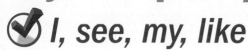

✔️ *I, see, my, like*

▶ Review

Give each small group the Word Cards, Picture Cards, and Punctuation Card needed to make a sentence. Each child holds one card. Children stand and arrange themselves to make a sentence for others to read.

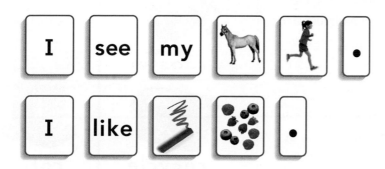

Repeat with other sentences.

▶ Apply

Practice Book page 102 Children can complete this page independently and read it to you during small group time.

Phonics Library Have children take turns reading aloud to the class. Each child might read one page of "Cat's Surprise" or a favorite **Phonics Library** selection from the previous theme. Remind readers to share the pictures!

- *Find pictures that start with the same sound as Nyle Noodle's name. What is the letter? What is the sound?*

- *Can you remember Mimi Mouse's sound? What is the letter? Can you find any pictures that begin with Mimi Mouse's sound in "Cat's Surprise?"*

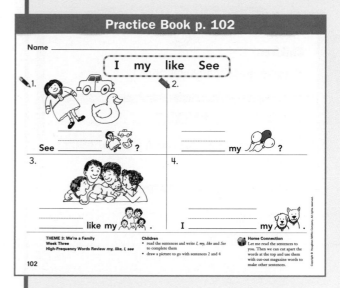

Practice Book p. 102

Portfolio Opportunity

Save the Practice Book page to show children's recognition of high-frequency words.

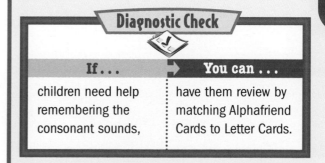

Diagnostic Check

If...	You can...
children need help remembering the consonant sounds,	have them review by matching Alphafriend Cards to Letter Cards.

DAY 5

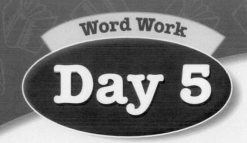

Day 5

Children

• explore environmental print

MATERIALS

• *From Apples to Zebras: A Book of ABC's,* page 19

Exploring Words

▶ ## Environmental Print

Recall with children that they have been talking about signs and words at school, in their neighborhoods, and at home that help them everyday.

■ Display *From Apples to Zebras: A Book of ABC's,* page 19. Remind children that this book shows the letters of the alphabet and some words that begin with these letters.

■ Page through the book with children, pausing for them to identify the example of environmental print. Ask: *Have you seen a sign (label) like this before? Where did you see it—at*

From Apples to Zebras: A Book of ABC's, page 19

home, at school, or in your neighborhood? How does this sign (label) help you?

Writing Opportunity Have children create signs for themselves by writing their names on sheets or strips of paper and decorating their names with pictures of things they like. Children can use their names to label their cubbies or another personal space in the classroom. If you have an instant camera, photograph each child. Children can include the pictures on their signs.

Independent Writing

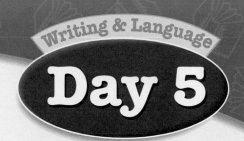

Journals Review this week's shared and interactive writing posted in the classroom. Point out the action words children listed and the directions they wrote. Discuss also what children learned and wrote about families. Explain that today children will write about something they learned.

- Pass out the journals.

- *This week we talked about signs and labels around our homes and neighborhood. We talked about action words that describe the things we do. What new words could you put in your journal?*

- *We also worked together to write directions. What order words did we use to write our directions?*

- Have children draw and write about something they learned this week. Remind them that they can refer to classroom charts, the Word Wall, and the Big Books as they write.

- Children will enjoy sharing what they've written with the class during meeting time.

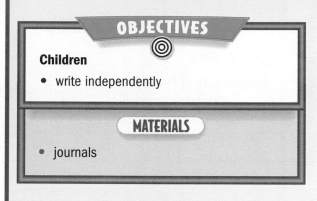

OBJECTIVES

Children
- write independently

MATERIALS
- journals

Portfolio Opportunity
Photocopy children's journals to show as examples of their writing growth.

walk

don't walk

DAY 5

Theme Assessment Wrap-Up

Emerging Literacy Survey

Areas Assessed:

1. Concepts of Print
- Letter name knowledge
- Sound-letter association

2. Phonemic Awareness
- Rhyme
- Beginning sounds
- Blending onsets and rimes
- Segmenting onsets and rimes
- Blending phonemes
- Segmenting phonemes

3. Beginning Reading and Writing
- Word recognition
- Word writing
- Sentence dictation
- Oral reading

▶ Monitoring Literacy Development

If you have administered the **Emerging Literacy Survey** as a baseline assessment of the skills children brought with them to Kindergarten, this might be a good time to re-administer all or part of it to chart progress, to identify areas of strength and need, and to test the need for early intervention.

Use the **Observation Checklist** throughout the theme to write notes indicating whether each child has a beginning, developing, or proficient understanding of reading, writing, and language concepts. (See facing page.)

▶ Assessing Student Progress

Formal Assessment The **Theme Skills Test** is a formal assessment used to evaluate children's performance on theme objectives.

■ The **Theme Skills Test** assesses children's mastery of specific reading and language arts skills taught in the theme.

Observation Checklist

Name _____ Date _____

	Beginning	Developing	Proficient
Listening Comprehension • Participates in shared and choral reading			
• Listens to story attentively			
Phonemic Awareness • Can identify beginning sounds			
Phonics • Can recognize initial sounds *t, b, n*			
Concepts of Print • Recognizes use of capital at the beginning of a sentence			
• Understands directionality: return sweep			
• Can identify end punctuation			
Reading • Can read wordless stories			
• Can read the high-frequency words *my, like*			
Comprehension • Identifies story structure: character/setting			
• Makes inferences: draws conclusions			
Writing and Language • Can write simple words			
• Can participate in shared and interactive writing			

For each child, write notes or checkmarks in the appropriate columns.

Theme Resources

Resources for *We're a Family*

Contents

Twinkle, Twinkle, Little Star

Use this music for Tiggy Tiger's song.

Three Blind Mice

Moderately

Party song

Use this music for Benny Bear's song.

The Farmer in the Dell

Lively

Use this music for Nyle Noodle's song.

Word List

In Themes 1 through 3, the Phonics Library stories are wordless.

Theme 1

▶ **Phonics Skills:** none taught in this theme
▶ **High-Frequency Words:** none taught in this theme

Phonics Library, Week 1:
We Go to School
　wordless story

Phonics Library, Week 2:
See What We Can Do
　wordless story

Phonics Library, Week 3:
We Can Make It
　wordless story

Theme 2

▶ **Phonics Skills:** Initial consonants s, m, r
▶ **High-Frequency Words:** I, see

Phonics Library, Week 1:
My Red Boat
　wordless story

Phonics Library, Week 2:
Look at Me
　wordless story

Phonics Library, Week 3:
The Parade
　wordless story

Theme 3

▶ **Phonics Skills:** Initial consonants t, b, n
▶ **High-Frequency Words:** my, like

Phonics Library, Week 1:
The Birthday Party
　wordless story

Phonics Library, Week 2:
Baby Bear's Family
　wordless story

Phonics Library, Week 3:
Cat's Surprise
　wordless story

Theme 4

▶ **Phonics Skills:** Initial consonants h, v, c; words with -at
▶ **High-Frequency Words:** a, to

Phonics Library, Week 1:
Nat at Bat
　Words with -at: at, bat, hat, Nat, sat
　High-Frequency Words: my, see

Phonics Library, Week 2:
A Vat
　Words with -at: hat, mat, rat, vat
　High-Frequency Word: a

Phonics Library, Week 3:
Cat Sat
　Words with -at: bat, cat, hat, mat, sat
　High-Frequency Words: my, see

Theme 5

▶ **Phonics Skills:** Initial consonants p, g, f; words with -an
▶ **High-Frequency Words:** and, go

Phonics Library, Week 1:
Nat, Pat, and Nan
　Words with -an: Nan, ran
　Words with -at: Nat, Pat, sat
　High-Frequency Words: and, see

Phonics Library, Week 2:
Go, Cat!
　Words with -an: Nan, ran, Van
　Words with -at: Cat, Pat, sat
　High-Frequency Word: go

Phonics Library, Week 3:
Pat and Nan
　Words with -an: fan, Nan, ran
　Words with -at: Pat, sat
　High-Frequency Words: a, and, go

Theme 6

▶ **Phonics Skills:** Initial consonants l, k, qu; words with -it
▶ **High-Frequency Words:** is, here

Phonics Library, Week 1:
Can It Fit?
　Words with -it: fit, it, sit
　Words with -an: can, man, van
　High-Frequency Words: a, go, I, is, my

Phonics Library, Week 2:
Kit
　Words with -it: bit, fit, it, Kit, lit, sit
　Words with -an: can, pan
　Words with -at: hat
　High-Frequency Words: a, here, I

Phonics Library, Week 3:
Fan
　Words with -it: bit, quit
　Words with -an: an, Fan
　Words with -at: sat
　High-Frequency Words: a, here, is

Theme 7

▶ **Phonics Skills:** Initial consonants d, z; words with -ig
▶ **High-Frequency Words:** for, have

Phonics Library, Week 1:
Big Rig
　Words with -ig: Big, dig, Rig
　Words with -it: pit
　Words with -an: can, Dan
　High-Frequency Words: a, for

Phonics Library, Week 2:
Tan Van
　Words with -ig: Pig, Zig
　Words with -it: it
　Words with -an: can, Dan, ran, tan, van
　Words with -at: Cat, sat
　High-Frequency Words: a, have, I, is

Phonics Library, Week 3:
Zig Pig and Dan Cat
　Words with -ig: dig, Pig, Zig
　Words with -it: it
　Words with -an: can, Dan
　Words with -at: Cat, sat
　High-Frequency Words: and, for, have, here, I, is

Theme 8

▶ **Phonics Skills:** Consonant x; words with -ot, -ox
▶ **High-Frequency Words:** said, the

Phonics Library, Week 1:
Dot Got a Big Pot
Words with -ot: Dot, got, hot, lot, pot
Words with -ig: big
Words with -it: it
Words with -an: Nan
Words with -at: Nat, sat
High-Frequency Words: a, and, I, is, like, said

Phonics Library, Week 2:
The Big, Big Box
Words with -ox: box, Fox
Words with -ot: not
Words with -ig: big
Words with -it: bit, fit, hit, it
Words with -an: can, Dan, Fan
Words with -at: Cat, hat, mat, sat
High-Frequency Words: a, is, my, said, the

Phonics Library, Week 3:
A Pot for Dan Cat
Words with -ot: pot
Words with -ox: Fox
Words with -ig: big
Words with -it: fit
Words with -an: can, Dan, Fan, ran
Words with -at: Cat, sat
High-Frequency Words: a, and, see, said

Theme 9

▶ **Phonics Skills:** Initial consonants w, y; words with -et, -en
▶ **High-Frequency Words:** play, she

Phonics Library, Week 1:
Get Set! Play!
Words with -et: get, set, wet, yet
Words with -ot: got, not
Words with -ox: Fox
Words with -ig: Pig
Words with -an: can
High-Frequency Words: a, play, said

Phonics Library, Week 2:
Ben
Words with -en: Ben, Hen, men, ten
Words with -et: get, net, pet, vet, yet
Words with -ot: got, not
Words with -ox: box, Fox
Words with -it: it
Words with -an: can
High-Frequency Words: a, I, my, play, said, she, the

Phonics Library, Week 3:
Pig Can Get Wet
Words with -et: get, wet
Words with -ot: got, not
Words with -ig: big, Pig, wig
Words with -it: sit
Words with -an: can
Words with -at: Cat, sat
High-Frequency Words: a, my, play, said, she

Theme 10

▶ **Phonics Skills:** Initial consonant j; words with -ug, -ut
▶ **High-Frequency Words:** are, he

Phonics Library, Week 1:
Ken and Jen
Words with -ug: dug
Words with -en: Ken, Jen
Words with -et: wet
Words with -ot: hot
Words with -ig: big, dig
Words with -it: it, pit
High-Frequency Words: a, and, are, is

Phonics Library, Week 2:
It Can Fit
Words with -ut: but, nut
Words with -ug: jug, lug, rug
Words with -ox: box
Words with -ot: not
Words with -ig: big
Words with -it: fit, it
Words with -an: can, tan, van
Words with -at: fat, hat
High-Frequency Words: a, he, see, she

Phonics Library, Week 3:
The Bug Hut
Words with -ut: but
Words with -ug: Bug, hug, lug
Words with -ox: box
Words with -ot: Dot, got, not
Words with -ig: Big, jig
Words with -an: can, Jan
Words with -at: fat, hat
High-Frequency Words: a, here, is, she, the

Cumulative Word List

By the end of Theme 10, children will have been taught the skills necessary to read the following words.

Words with -at
at, bat, cat, fat, hat, mat, Nat, Pat, rat, sat, vat

Words with -an
an, ban, can, Dan, fan, Jan, man, Nan, pan, ran, tan, van

Words with -it
bit, fit, hit, it, kit, lit, pit, quit, sit, wit

Words with -ig
big, dig, fig, jig, pig, rig, wig, zig

Words with -ot
cot, dot, got, hot, jot, lot, not, pot, rot, tot

Words with -ox
box, fox, ox

Words with -et
bet, get, jet, let, met, net, pet, set, vet, wet, yet

Words with -en
Ben, den, hen, Jen, Ken, men, pen, ten

Words with -ug
bug, dug, hug, jug, lug, mug, rug, tug

Words with -ut
but, cut, hut, jut, nut, rut

High-Frequency Words
a, and, are, for, go, have, he, here, I, is, like, my, play, said, see, she, the, to

Technology Resources

American Melody
P. O. Box 270
Guilford, CT 06473
800-220-5557

Audio Bookshelf
174 Prescott Hill Road
Northport, ME 04849
800-234-1713

Baker & Taylor
100 Business Court Drive
Pittsburgh, PA 15205
800-775-2600

BDD Audio
1540 Broadway
New York, NY 10036
800-223-6834

Big Kids Productions
1606 Dwyer Avenue
Austin, TX 78704
800-477-7811
www.bigkidsvideo.com

Blackboard Entertainment
2647 International
Boulevard
Suite 853
Oakland, CA 94601
800-968-2261
www.blackboardkids.com

Books on Tape
P. O. Box 7900
Newport Beach, CA 92658
800-626-3333

Filmic Archives
The Cinema Center
Botsford, CT 06404
800-366-1920
www.filmicarchives.com

Great White Dog Picture Company
10 Toon Lane
Lee, NH 03824
800-397-7641
www.greatwhitedog.com

HarperAudio
10 E. 53rd Street
New York, NY 10022
800-242-7737

Houghton Mifflin Company
222 Berkeley Street
Boston, MA 02116
800-225-3362

Informed Democracy
P. O. Box 67
Santa Cruz, CA 95063
831-426-3921

JEF Films
143 Hickory Hill Circle
Osterville, MA 02655
508-428-7198

Kimbo Educational
P. O. Box 477
Long Branch, NJ 07740
900-631-2187

The Learning Company (dist. for Broderbund)
1 Athenaeum Street
Cambridge, MA 02142
800-716-8506
www.learningco.com

Library Video Co.
P. O. Box 580
Wynnewood, PA 19096
800-843-3620

Listening Library
One Park Avenue
Old Greenwich, CT 06870
800-243-45047

Live Oak Media
P. O. Box 652
Pine Plains, NY 12567
800-788-1121
liveoak@taconic.net

Media Basics
Lighthouse Square
P. O. Box 449
Guilford, CT 06437
800-542-2505
www.mediabasicsvideo.com

Microsoft Corp.
One Microsoft Way
Redmond, WA 98052
800-426-9400
www.microsoft.com

National Geographic Society
1145 17th Street N. W.
Washington, D. C. 20036
800-368-2728
www.nationalgeographic.com

New Kid Home Video
1364 Palisades Beach Road
Santa Monica, CA 90401
310-451-5164

Puffin Books
345 Hudson Street
New York, NY 10014
212-366-2000

Rainbow Educational Media
4540 Preslyn Drive
Raleigh, NC 27616
800-331-4047

Random House Home Video
201 E. 50th Street
New York, NY 10022
212-940-7620

Recorded Books
270 Skipjack Road
Prince Frederick, MD 20678
800-638-1304
www.recordedbooks.com

Sony Wonder
Dist. by Professional
Media Service
19122 S. Vermont Avenue
Gardena, CA 90248
800-223-7672

Spoken Arts
8 Lawn Avenue
P. O. Box 100
New Rochelle, NY 10802
800-326-4090

SRA Media
220 E. Danieldale Road
DeSoto, TX 75115
800-843-8855

Sunburst Communications
101 Castleton Street
P. O. Box 100
Pleasantville, NY 10570
800-321-7511
www.sunburst.com

SVE & Churchill Media
6677 North Northwest
Highway
Chicago, IL 60631
800-829-1900

Tom Snyder Productions
80 Coolidge Hill Road
Watertown, MA 02472
800-342-0236
www.tomsnyder.com

Troll Communications
100 Corporate Drive
Mahwah, NJ 07430
800-526-5289

Weston Woods
12 Oakwood Avenue
Norwalk, CT 06850-1318
800-243-5020
www.scholastic.com

Index

Boldface page references indicate formal strategy and skill instruction.

Emergent writing
draw/write to record information, *T25, T39, T46, T102*

English Language Learners, activities especially helpful for, *T42, T64, T98, T120*
background, building, *T10*

Environmental print
signs, *T144, T152, T160*

Evaluating literature. *See* Literature, evaluating.

F

Fluency
reading, *T51, T107*

G

Grammar and usage
sentence, parts of a
naming part, *T71*
speech, parts of. *See* Speech, parts of.

Graphic information, interpreting
calendars, *T8, T16, T26, T40, T48, T62, T72, T82, T96, T104, T118, T128, T138, T146, T154*
pictures, *T19*

Guided reading. *See* Coached reading.

H

Handwriting, *T21, T77, T133*

High-frequency words
I, **T14, T53, T70, T109, T159**
like, **T78–T79, T109, T134–T135, T159**
my, **T22–T23, T26, T48, T53, T70, T109, T134–T135, T159**
see, **T14, T53, T70, T109, T159**

Home connection, *xiii, T12, T37, T44, T51, T68, T100, T107, T124, T143, T150, T157*

I

Independent writing, *T55, T111, T161*

Individual needs, meeting
Challenge, *T33, T81, T99, T149*
English Language Learners, *T10, T42, T64, T98, T120*
Extra Support, *T19, T20, T28, T36, T43, T75, T76, T84, T92, T99, T132, T140, T142, T148*

Inferences, making
drawing conclusions, *T64, T74, T86, T87, T88, T98, T106, T120, T140, T141, T148, T149*

Informational selection, structure of. *See* Comprehension skills, text organization.

Interactive writing, *T40, T47, T48, T62, T72, T103, T153, T154*

J

Journal, *T38, T47, T55, T111, T161*

L

Language and usage. *See* Grammar and usage.

Language concepts and skills
language patterns, *T88*

Language games, *xiv, T49*

Leveled books
Houghton Mifflin Classroom Bookshelf, *T51, T107, T157*
Little Big Books, *T51, T107, T157*
Little Readers for Guided Reading, *T51, T107, T157*
On My Way Practice Reader, *T157*
Phonics Library, *iv, v, T37, T45, T53, T93, T107, T109, T143, T151, T159*

Limited English proficient students. *See* English Language Learners.

Listening
purpose
to compare sounds, *T45, T63, T69, T92*
to discriminate sounds, *T17, T125*
to an audiotape. *See* Audiotapes.
to a read aloud story. *See* Read Aloud selections.
to riddles, *T12, T68*

Literature
comparing, *T50, T106*
discussion. *See* Responding to literature.
evaluating, *T86, T87, T88, T98, T131, T140, T149*
responding to. *See* Responding to literature.
sharing, *T18–T19, T28–T32, T42–T43, T74–T75, T84–T89, T98–T99, T130–T131, T140–T141, T148–T149*

M

Mechanics, language. *See* Concepts of print.

Modeling
student, *T31, T32, T42, T86, T87, T88, T98, T130, T140*
teacher, *T10, T18, T64, T74, T120*
teacher-student, *T29, T85, T86*
writing, *T8, T16, T26, T82, T96, T104, T118, T128, T138, T146*

Monitoring comprehension. See Strategies, reading.

Multi-age classroom, *xii*

N

Newsletters. *See* Home connection.

Nouns. *See* Speech, parts of.

T

Teacher-guided reading. *See* Coached reading; Reading modes.

Teacher's Note, *xiv, T6, T21, T24, T32, T33, T61, T65, T77, T88, T116, T121, T133*

Teaching and management
   special needs of students, meeting. *See* Individual needs, meeting.

Technology resources, *xiii, T50, T106, T156, R8*

Text organization and structure. *See* Comprehension skills.

Theme, launching the, *xii–xiii*

Theme projects, *xiii*

Think Aloud. *See* Modeling, teacher.

U

Usage. *See* Grammar and usage.

V

Viewing activities
   illustrations. *See* Picture clues.

Vocabulary, extending
   action words, *T127*
   clothing words, *T71, T72, T80, T81*
   days of the week, *T8, T16, T40, T48, T62, T82, T138*
   definitions, *T42*
   family words, *T25, T38, T46, T54, T94, T102, T110*
   holidays, *T54*
   movement words, *T15*
   order words, *T137, T145, T153*
   rhyming words, *T40*
   See also Language concepts and skills.

Vocabulary, selection
   high-frequency words. *See* High-frequency words.

W

Word wall, *T8, T16, T22, T26, T40, T48, T62, T72, T78, T82, T96, T104, T118, T128, T134, T138, T146, T154*

Writer's log. *See* Journal.

Writing activities and types
   cooperative writing. *See* Shared writing.
   diaries, logs, and notebooks. *See* Journal.
   emergent. *See* Emergent writing.
   independent. *See* Independent writing.
   interactive. *See* Interactive writing.
   letters and cards, *T54*
   lists, *T95, T103*
   signs, *T160*

Writing skills
   formats. *See* Writing activities.
   language and writing
      action words, **T127**
   prewriting skills
      drawing, **T7, T35, T46, T71, T94**
   title, writing a, **T103**
   record information/observation, **T39**